TREASURES
OF
DENMARK

FROM THE VIKINGS TO NOW

BY
PATRICK HOWARTH

Consultant:
Hans–Jørgen Frederiksen
Head of Department of History, Aarhus University.

Eric Dobby Publishing

Published by
Eric Dobby Publishing Ltd
12 Warnford Road
Orpington, Kent BR6 6LW
England

ISBN 1-85882-050-2 *(Hardback)*
ISBN 1-85882-053-7 *(Paperback)*

Designed in Denmark by Contrapunkt
Electronic Artwork by Graphic Examples
Printed in the European Union

CONTENTS

To Britt and Lone

Britt S. Lightbody
The Danish Tourist Board, London

Lone Britt Christensen
The Royal Danish Embassy, London

ACKNOWLEDGEMENTS

I owe a deep debt to Hans-Jørgen Frederiksen, Head of the Art History Department at Aarhus University, who at an early stage agreed to act as consultant for this book and has guided me throughout. I was also much helped by his colleagues, Bob Jacobsen, librarian and Torben Nielsen, photographer.

I am much indebted too to Lone Britt Christensen of the Danish Embassy and Britt Sander Lightbody of the Danish Tourist Board in London, who actively supported this project from its inception.

I am considerably indebted too to Paul Cederdorff for guidance.

Of the experts who gave me much of their valuable time I wish particularly to thank Ebbe Nyborg of the National Museum, Peter Larsen of the National Museum of Fine Arts, Tove Vejlstrup of the Louisiana Museum of Modern Art, Soren Dietz and Claus Grenne of the Ny Carlsberg Glyptotek, Lene Lund Feveile of the Ribe Viking Museum, Dr Ulla Hønkjær of the Industrial Art Museum, Peter Kristiansen of Rosenborg Castle, Erik Westengaard of Frederiksborg Castle, Gertrud Witt of the Thorvaldsen Museum, Professor Carsten Thau of the Royal Academy School of Architecture, Steen Nokelmann of Royal Copenhagen Porcelain and Ulf Steenbjoern, architect.

For the rest there are so many people in Denmark whom I wish to thank that it is difficult to decide where to begin and where to end.

Perhaps I should begin by thanking the management of the Radisson SAS hotels in Denmark, from which I emerged day after day in search of treasures of Denmark. I even discovered, as I point out in the final chapters of this book, that more than one of the hotels are among the architectural treasures.

Among the many others who helped me in different ways I would like to thank the following, listed in alphabetical order: Susanne Andersen, Connie Bach, Ann Marie Barsøe, Tina Bladbjerg, Karen Grøn, Andrew Guest, Bent Hansen, Merete Hegner, Hennis Hytteballe, Rev Anne Hvild, Anne Marie Ravn Jensen, Jørn Grønkjær Jensen, Birgit Jenvold, Anna Kjær, Peter Kristiansen, Leila Krogh, Esben Larsen, Dr Henning Larsen, Ib Larsen, Inger Lauridsen, Gitte Madsen, Monica Ritterband, Charlotte Sahl-Madsen, Dr Michael Sorensen-Jones, Ole Schjøning, Olaf Sielemann, Anne Westh, Barbara Whitworth and John Zilmer.

I have received valuable help from tourist offices in all parts of Denmark. To mention the names of all those who assisted me in various ways would produce an excessively long list. I hope, instead, my various benefactors in these offices will accept from me a comprehensive expression of thanks.

Most of all I owe a debt to my wife Eva, who did so much to bring this book into being.

I.

THE VIKING VISION

"Aboard, aboard. The wind sits in the shoulder of your sail" - Polonius, Hamlet

TREFOIL BRONZE BROOCH
NATIONAL MUSEUM
COPENHAGEN

Wherever you go in Denmark you cannot be more than sixty kilometres from the sea. Not surprisingly the influence of the sea is apparent in much of the greatest visual art which Danes have created in the last thousand years.

Bridges, which, from a distance, seem to have been constructed of gossamer, link Denmark's islands. Fortified castles constructed as a defence against invaders from the sea were replaced by Renaissance palaces. Some of Denmark's most gifted artists came together at Skagen to paint the peculiar light off North Jutland, where the Baltic and North Seas meet.

If you enter a Danish church you may well see a beautifully carved ship's model suspended from the ceiling. Ships in medieval frescoes transport ancient kings

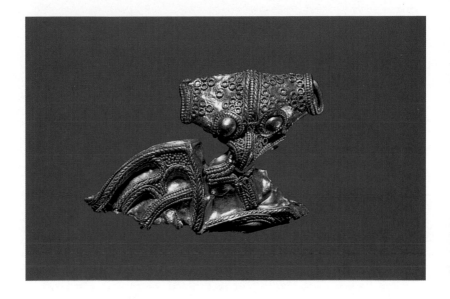

and warriors. A familiar artefact of the
Royal Copenhagen factory is a porcelain
seagull. To the outside world the symbol
of the city of Copenhagen is a mermaid
carved in stone. But at no time was the
sea more important to the nation's art
than in the Viking age, and an essential
ingredient of that art was the ship.

Viking ships were intrinsically beautiful
objects, and the ways in which they were
decorated indicates the pride their
builders and owners felt in them. They
were depicted in a variety of art forms,
and they had a place of importance in
Viking religion and folk-lore.

Fortunately a number of Viking ships
have been recovered in various states of
preservation. The richest Danish
maritime treasure from the Viking age
was found near Roskilde. As a defensive

strategy five ships had been scuttled in the late Viking age with the object of denying passage to an enemy through Roskilde fjord. These were excavated in 1962 and today can be seen, admirably displayed, in the Roskilde Viking Ship Museum. Two of the vessels were warships, two were cargo ships, and one was probably a fishing boat. By their very variety they give an illuminating insight into Viking maritime life and ship-building methods, although not all were of Danish construction.

The first impression of the unprepared visitor is likely to be of wonder at slenderness and beauty of curved line. These qualities are particularly evident in the warships. They had a narrow beam and continuous full-length decking. They were built for speed, had a full complement of oars, and could operate almost independently of the wind. The mast could be easily lowered and raised, which was an asset when making surprise attacks. They had a shallow draft and thin planking and could be run ashore on beaches and on river banks in estuaries. Indeed the Vikings seem to have been reluctant to bring their ships alongside a waterfront or another ship, no doubt thinking that only in such situations would they be vulnerable.

Cargo ships were broader in the beam than warships. They depended mainly on a single square sail, oars being used when the ship was becalmed or for

manoeuvring close to shore. A smaller
crew could be carried than that needed
for the warships, in which everyone had
to be both mariner and fighting man. Yet
to those who see excavated Viking cargo
ships in Roskilde or other Danish Viking
museums it may seem astonishing that
these vessels were deemed large enough
to transport numerous horses and sheep
in addition to their other cargo. That
horses were carried in Viking ships is
attested by pictures in tapestries such as
the famous Bayeux work.

The Vikings' cargo ships were, no less
than their warships, superb examples of
craftsmanship. To the modern craftsman it
may seem astonishing that both
categories of ship were built without the
use of a saw.

The shipwrights had the advantage of
access to large numbers of tall forest oaks
with straight grain of a kind not readily

PAINTING OF A VIKING SHIP
BY FLEMMING BAU.
WITH A CREW OF BETWEEN
60 AND 100 WARRIORS, OAK-
BUILT, SHE WAS SOME 30
METRES IN LENGTH AND HAD
A DISPLACEMENT OF ABOUT
16 TONS
THE VIKING SHIPS MUSEUM
ROSKILDE

found today. They would choose timber whose grain followed as closely as possible that of the pieces required. The beautiful curved stems both fore and aft would be made from a single piece.

It has been estimated that about eleven trees were needed for a warship some 20-25 metres in length. The timber would be hewn by axe, knives and chisels. Hammers were also used. Other raw materials included iron nails, pine tar for waterproofing, skins of walrus or seals and wool for the sails.

In vessels fashioned in this manner Vikings, in the words of a French monk writing in the eleventh century, "placing their confidence in such a fleet, when the signal was given, set out gladly and, as they had been ordered, placed themselves round about the royal vessel. The blue water, smitten by many oars, might be seen foaming far and wide, and the sunlight, cast back in the gleam of metal, spread a double radiance in the air."

We can readily take pleasure today in the beauty of line of Viking ships even after they have been under water or land for centuries. The same cannot be said of many of the decorative and symbolic features which they once had. Of these the French monk wrote: ". . . Lions moulded in gold were to be seen on the ships, birds on the tops of the masts indicated by their movements the winds as they blew, or dragons of various kinds poured fire from their nostrils. Here there were glittering men of solid gold or silver nearly comparable to live ones, there bulls with necks raised high and legs outstretched were fashioned leaping and roaring." Dolphins and centaurs were among the other creatures moulded or embossed.

From a variety of descriptions by contemporaries or in sagas we learn that prows and sterns were carved in the shapes of animals and covered in gold - presumably gilded copper - and that the rest of the ship was painted. One account in a saga tells of square sails striped or chequered in red, blue, green and white.

Ships were depicted in Scandinavian art as early as the Bronze Age, and in their wood and stone carvings, their paintings, their jewellery and metalwork the Vikings continued the practice. As means of transport to the after-life ships had an obvious place in religious beliefs and, consequently, in ceremonial. In 1935 remnants of a Viking ship, 22 metres in length, were excavated at Ladby near Nyborg. She had been hauled ashore a thousand years earlier to serve as the burial chamber of a man of evident importance. With him had been buried eleven horses, four dogs and various valuable objects, including a solid silver buckle with leaf patterns on both sides, which is thought to have been of Frankish origin. To enable him, presumably, to continue hunting and otherwise amusing himself after death there were also some arrows, a silver-plated whip and a gaming board.

The Viking age, it is generally agreed, extended from about the beginning of the ninth century to the middle of the eleventh. Throughout this time there was an outpouring of skilled seamen and warriors from Denmark, Norway and Sweden. Other Europeans applied the term "Viking" to all Scandinavians, even though by the end of the Viking age there were three distinct Scandinavian kingdoms.

The first Vikings to make an impact on other European countries were pirates and raiders. Understandably they attacked monasteries, for they soon learnt of the riches to be found in them, including quantities of wine. The loot that was available and the stories that were told inspired more and more men to seek their fortunes outside

THE VIKING CRAFTS OF SHIP-BUILDING AS PORTRAYED IN THE BAYEUX TAPESTRIES.

Scandinavia, and in time the Vikings became traders rather than raiders. Some became colonists, populating Iceland and founding, for example, the city of Dublin. Many of the Vikings returned home and brought with them evidence, sometimes startling, of the arts and crafts of Europe, Asia Minor and North Africa. After a time the cultural traffic became increasingly two-way.

Among the items which Danes and other Vikings exported were amber, furs, narwhal ivory and, as a consequence of raiding, slaves. Imports included glass, pottery and metalwork, particular importance being attached to swords, some of them highly decorated. Large quantities of silver were also transported for the payment of danegeld - payments made to dissuade Danes from carrying out acts of war. These payments were normally transacted in silver.

Danes settled predominantly in England, and recent archaeological discoveries have much increased the respect felt for the arts and crafts which they evidently practised there. In time Danes became so powerful that they even provided England with kings. Indeed the very concept of a kingdom of England was to some extent of Danish origin.

That the Vikings were able to make the impact they did was largely due to their mastery of the sea. In an earlier age an otherwise undistinguished people, the Huns, had been able to advance from the borders of China deep into the empires of Persia and Rome because of their supreme mastery of one form of transport, the horse. The Vikings had a comparable mastery of the ocean-going vessel. It was a skill which was to bring them in organised bodies to Alexandria and Byzantium in one direction, in another to Greenland and, beyond, to the shores of North America.

The Vikings, like their ancestors, were imaginative people, as their mythology makes clear. Only an imaginative people could have conceived and worshipped such a god as Odin, who exchanged the use of one eye for the privilege of drinking from the well of wisdom, who rode an eight-legged horse and was the god of poetry. His son, the red-bearded Thor, rode through the sky in a chariot drawn by two sacred goats. When he passed by thunder and lightning were experienced on earth.

The quality of vivid imagination is evident in much that survives of the Vikings' visual arts. These arts were highly stylised, largely non-representational, and ornamental. The objects ornamented were for the most part those in everyday use. They included, in addition to jewellery, waggons and sledges, swords and spears, harnesses, bridles and stirrups. Some impression of the number of craftsmen engaged in such work and the manner in which they operated can be formed today in Ribe, where the ancient market-place has been reconstructed and potters and grinders, basket-makers and

GOLDEN NECK RING
A FARMER WORKING IN A FIELD NEAR TISSØ IN ZEALAND FOUND AN OBJECT NEAR HIS SOWING MACHINE. THIS LED TO THE GREATEST DISCOVERY OF GOLD TREASURE EVER MADE IN DENMARK. THE GOLD RING MUST HAVE ORIGINALLY WEIGHED OVER 2 KILOS AND WOULD, IT IS THOUGHT, HAVE PURCHASED AT LEAST 500 CATTLE
NATIONAL MUSEUM COPENHAGEN

GRIPPING BEASTS, FAMILIAR
MOTIFS IN VIKING ART

DRAWINGS
THE VIKING SHIPS MUSEUM
ROSKILDE

weavers, smiths and bow-makers can be seen at work.

Much of Viking ornamental art took the form of carving and painting on wood, unfortunately little of the wood has survived. One revealing piece excavated in Hørning shows a carving of a black-painted snake, whose eye is painted red. It is in what has survived in gold, silver, amber, stone and other enduring substances, that Viking visual arts are largely to be enjoyed.

The most startling of the creatures the Vikings depicted is surely the so-called "gripping beast." This evidently caught the imagination of a number of artists, for it appears in various art-forms. It is immediately recognisable by its paws, which clutch at other animals or inanimate objects, at itself or at the border of a design. Other characteristics are a broad grin, large ears, a long pigtail and short legs. The paws are massive in relation to other parts of its body. In one pair of Danish brooches dating from the ninth century the gripping beast even seems to be throttling itself. Why this beast should have appeared in the art forms of Denmark, and indeed of the other Scandinavian countries, is an abiding and intriguing mystery. So too, it may be thought, is the rarity of the human form as a source of inspiration.

Scholars have fairly recently begun to classify Viking art by periods, a system based largely on a number of important archaeological finds. Generally speaking, the art styles revealed were common to all the Scandinavian countries. Many of the finds are from the graves of evidently rich people, and it is possible to determine the date of burial fairly accurately. The earliest of these finds were at Oseberg in Norway, which include magnificent wood carvings from early Viking times.

GOLD BROOCH

NATIONAL MUSEUM

COPENHAGEN

In the style represented by the finds in Borre in Sweden ring-chain patterns are common, and it is evident that there were craftsmen who were masters of the technique of filigree and granulation. Examples of Borre-style work have emerged in countries as far apart as Russia and Ireland. The two great archaeological finds in Denmark were in Jelling and Mammen. Discoveries at the

royal burial ground at Jelling include what is believed to be the burial
chamber of King Gorm the Old. If so its construction must date from
the mid-tenth century.

Among the finds is a small silver cup decorated with the intertwining
bodies of two animals. Heads are shown in profile and jaws are open.
Other features are a curling upper lip, a pigtail and a circular hip-joint.
The ribbon-like bodies are decorated with a ladder-pattern. The human
form does appear in Jelling finds, notably in a carved red and yellow
wooden figure, but as this has been bound in a manner similar to that of
the body of Christ, it may be reasonable to assume that Christian practice
has already been grafted on to Viking tradition.

Another object in the Jelling style, which was found at Søllested on Fyn,
is a harness bow cast in bronze and richly decorated. At the extremities
are two voracious creatures holding the metal in their mouths. Facing
them are two other animals placed back to back, and in the centre is a
panel containing two tiny human figures. The viewer could spend hours
in tracing the intricacy of the patterns and guessing the identity of the
animals and humans.

The Mammen style has much in common with the Jelling style and
follows it fairly closely in time. One important respect in which it differs
is the increasing use of foliate motifs. Jelling-style animals have small
embellishments in the form of tendrils. In the Mammen style the
influence of mainland Europe, where acanthus leaves, for example, were
common forms of ornament, is clearly evident. One of the most
impressive works of art in the Mammen style is a decorated battle-axe.
On one side birds and a human mask can be seen. The reverse side is
given up to a variety of intertwining forms of foliage.

The other two major finds, at Ringerike and at Urnes in Norway, are of
late Viking work. Although the curves and the intricate patterns continue
to form the basis of much of the art, there is a greater realism in the
depiction of animals. A weather-vane on the prow of an eleventh century
Viking ship found at Ringerike, for example, is surmounted by a four-
footed creature not unlike a dog, though beneath and behind are more
traditional mythological animals engaged in combat. In the Urnes style

the impact of Christianity can already be
seen. This is represented in spectacular
form in church sculpture. The
characteristic pattern is made up of
curving and interlaced lines of different
widths, giving an effect of grace and
elegance.

For the full enjoyment of all this Viking
art, time and effort are needed. A
superficial glance may suggest a number
of abstract designs to which no meaning
can be attributed. A closer look reveals
creatures which cannot be identified
zoologically. The next stage of
understanding may come when the head
of an animal has been spotted. It is then
possible to follow its sinuous body,
intertwined perhaps with foliage, another
animal or itself. As understanding dawns
the viewer may well feel privileged by
being confronted with art of
extraordinary originality.

Although much of the best Viking art
that survives was executed on objects of
practical use, there is plenty of surviving
evidence of how the services of artists
were engaged for purely decorative
work. Amber, a Baltic product, continued

JELLING STYLE

MAMMEN STYLE

URNES STYLE

DRAWINGS
THE VIKING SHIPS MUSEUM
ROSKILDE

RUNESTONE

NATIONAL MUSEUM

COPENHAGEN

DETAIL FROM JELLING STONE

to be used, as it had been for centuries, for the making of beads, pendants and other forms of ornamentation. It was deemed to be endowed with mystical qualities, and some Viking warriors adorned themselves with amber bears to give them extra courage. Narwhal ivory was another indigenous product inviting the attention of artists and craftsmen.

Gold and silver - imported of course - while serving as bullion in the absence of coinage, were widely used for objects which were both decorative and functional. Among silver finds have been neck-rings, arm-rings and finger-rings, brooches and pendants.

Viking women of wealth and importance wore brooches on both shoulders as fasteners holding up their dresses. Some of these, cast in bronze, were oval in shape and decorated with stylised animal figures. A shawl or cloak would be fastened by a third brooch. They might be ornamented with gold or silver filigree, and beads might be suspended between the shoulder-brooches. Men also fastened their cloaks this way, one striking Danish example depicting the heads of two heavily moustached Vikings.

Ear-rings seem to have been a rarity, but women commonly wore rings round the neck. One Arab writer stated that a Viking man's wealth could be measured by the number of his wife's gold or silver rings.

A study of Viking art in Denmark must be conducted largely in museums, where numerous objects are rewardingly displayed. But some impression of what was created may also be had as a result of commercial enterprise. This has been the fashioning with scrupulous care of copies of Viking ornaments in gold, silver and bronze, which are now sold through shops.

Weaving as an art form was certainly practised, but of the tapestries the Vikings are known to have created little remains. Stone, by contrast, is an enduring substance, and in it the Vikings – and indeed their predecessors – created objects and designs of abiding interest.

JELLING STONE SHOWING
CHRIST FIGURE
DRAWING
THE VIKING SHIPS MUSEUM
ROSKILDE

The Viking form of writing known as
runes is of considerable antiquity,
Some runestones were decorated with
pictorial art of a kind which is
unmistakably Viking. The vertical bands,
the snakes, the dragons are all to be
found. A runestone discovered in Lund
shows two animals with geometric
patterns on their bodies fighting either
with their tongues or with swords. In
other runestones Viking warriors are
portrayed brandishing circular shields and
standing on the bodies of their dogs.

The most famous of all the Danish stones
is of exceptional interest both artistically
and historically. This is the memorial
stone of the ruler known as Gorm the
Old, which was erected in Jelling. In this
a large animal is depicted, with foliage
serving as his crest and tail, struggling
with a snake, whose body is entwined
around itself. The inscription reads:

VIKING AGE BROOCH
MOESGAARD MUSEUM

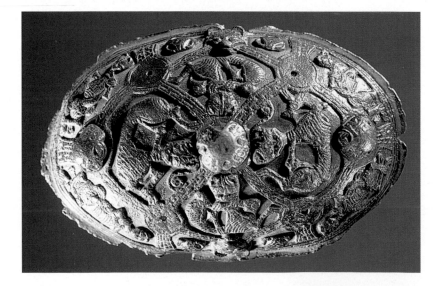

"King Harald commanded this
monument to be made in memory of
Gorm, his father, and in memory of
Thorvi, his mother, the Harald who won
the whole of Denmark for himself, and
Norway, and made the Danes Christian."

It was making the Danes Christian which
effectively brought Viking art to an end.
Established art forms do not of course
vanish overnight. Some of the best
Viking-style art was executed after
Harald Bluetooth's famous act of
conversion. The gripping beast gives way
to a slim, greyhound-type creature. There
is a new delicacy in silver brooches and
fluted silver bowls. Elegance was both
sought after and achieved. But deeper
changes would soon come about.

In their travels Danes had absorbed
much. In particular they had been deeply
impressed by such sights and sounds as
cathedrals built in stone, church
vestments and church music. In time
missionaries came to Denmark to preach
the gospel which gave rise to such
creations. The missionaries were made
welcome by kings, and resident bishops
were installed.

A great age of church building followed.
The hammer of the god Thor was
replaced by the cross. But for some time
to come traces of Viking styles could be
seen in the new and, no doubt, intensely
exciting Christian art.

II.

MEDIEVAL RICHES

"Let thine eye look like a friend on Denmark" – Gertrude, Hamlet

A traveller through Denmark today may well observe that farm buildings and dwellings seem, for the most part, to have been constructed in conformity with the flat terrain. Rising above them are slender windmills and, more conspicuously, white painted medieval parish churches surmounted by towers which seem to have stepping-stones leading up to heaven.

To anyone who delights in visiting churches Denmark offers exceptional riches. These riches were nearly all created during two periods of the nation's history, the medieval and the modern. Medieval Denmark had more than 2,700 parish churches in addition to about 140 monasteries, convents and cathedrals. This was the outcome of an extraordinary upsurge of faith and artistic creativity in a country to which Christianity came late.

ÅBY CRUCIFIX
NATIONAL MUSEUM,
COPENHAGEN

Happily, a considerable number of the churches remain in a condition which allows the perceptive visitor with a little imagination to picture them largely as they were when the first men and women worshipped there. An authoritative survey has shown the number of extant Danish churches of Romanesque origin to be 1,644. It may not be an exaggeration to suggest that these 1,644 churches are among the principal reasons why the discerning traveller should choose to visit Denmark.

The first known Christian missionary to Denmark, Ansgar of Hamburg, arrived as late as 826. King Harald Bluetooth's conversion occurred about 960. A hundred years later the chronicler known as Adam of Bremen wrote that there were about 150 churches in Zealand. It was in the two centuries which followed that the first great age of Danish church building occurred.

By the middle of the thirteenth century nearly every parish in Denmark had its own solidly built church. Some of the towns were even more favoured. Medieval Roskilde, for example, with only a few thousand inhabitants, had a cathedral, thirteen parish churches, five monasteries, a hospital of the Order of the Holy Spirit, a leper-house and three chapels.

Most of the early churches were built of wood. In contrast with Norway, where stave churches are still to be seen in appreciable numbers, the Danish wooden churches have vanished except as archaeological finds. The first Danish stone church, which evidently replaced an earlier wooden one, is believed to have been built in Roskilde about 1030.

For some time builders in Denmark were dependent on the local materials available. In Jutland the principal stone was granite, which is hard and unyielding. The early church builders used granite rubble picked up from the fields, where it had been deposited during the Ice Age, selecting those stones which had a comparatively flat surface. Such Ice Age relics remain today a feature of the Jutland countryside.

Their Viking predecessors had created the beautiful lines of their ships without the use of a saw. Early medieval stone-masons in Jutland overcame comparable difficulties with comparable skills, continuing to build in granite through the thirteenth century. Fortunately, as a material for building exterior walls granite can be formidably impressive, as a number of Jutland's Romanesque churches show.

In Zealand and elsewhere there were churches built of limestone and of calcareous tufa. According to legend, tufa was transformed from sea foam in answer to the prayers of St Knud, who wished to fill Zealand with churches. The earliest examples of brick building in Danish churches date from the middle of the twelfth century. The bricks are believed to have

been introduced from Lombardy through monastic connections.

Danish Romanesque churches, as originally built, were for the most part simple structures, consisting only of a nave, a chancel and a square or rounded apse. In some of the churches there was a gallery of the same width as the nave, which served as a pew for the leading local family, who may well have paid for the building.

There were flat timber roofs, and light filtered through round-arched, small windows of the kind found in Romanesque churches in many European countries. A few of the

churches had a low window in the south
wall, known as a lepers' window, the
assumption being that lepers would
thereby be able to witness the service
and receive the host by proxy.

Among the most interesting exceptions
to the standard style of building are some
round churches built on the island of
Bornholm. Four of these were
constructed in the second half of the
twelfth century. On an island frequently
threatened by invasion they clearly served
three distinct purposes: worship, storage
and defence. The ground floor, with a
central pillar and startling frescoes,
offered sanctuary as well as opportunities
for divine service. Grain and other
necessities for a siege were kept on the

ØSTERLARS CHURCH
BORNHOLM

second floor. From the top floor arrows could be fired at invaders. With their rounded shape, whitewashed exteriors and black, cone-shaped roofs, the churches are suggestive in appearance of the oasthouses in south-east England.

Bornholm has granite cliffs, some of which have a striking, sculpted appearance. The oldest of the round churches, and arguably the most beautiful, the Olsker church, is of granite construction, a man-made supplement to the cliffs fashioned in the Ice Age.

A church which is something of a curiosity, having been designed to emphasise class distinction, was built in the thirteenth century at Ledøje in Zealand, not far from Copenhagen. Its form was decided by an immigrant

German, Conrad of Reginstein, to a pattern he knew from his homeland. In effect there are two churches, one on the upper floor for the nobility, the other on the ground floor for the common people.

Some of the monastic churches are rather more complex, having a number of additional altars. In Veng church in Jutland, for example, in addition to the extra storey on the west side for the land-owning family, there were storeys on the north and the south for the use of the monks. According to Benedictine rules, all the priests had to say mass at least once a day. For this reason in Veng six extra altars were provided.

As knowledge of Gothic styles was passed on from the European mainland changes were made to the parish churches. With the plentiful supply of existing churches there was little need for new ones. Instead, when extensions or repairs were needed they were carried out in Gothic style. Hence the many surviving Danish Romanesque parish churches with strikingly Gothic modifications and additions.

Internally the changes most commonly introduced were extensions of chancel and nave, the replacement of wooden ceilings by rib vaulting, which greatly increased the height of the building, and the addition of chapels and sacristies. Some of the chapels served to house altars donated by the pious, others were baptismal chapels. In a number of churches, as a consequence of the changes, brick superstructures can be seen resting on the original stone bases.

Perhaps the change which makes the greatest impact today was the replacing of some of the small rounded Romanesque windows with much taller pointed Gothic ones, which served to flood the once darkened churches with light.

On the outside the most evident changes were the additions of towers and porches. Romanesque churches had two doorways, one for men on the south side, and the other, in the north, for women. It was an arrangement which invited draughts and with obvious disadvantages in the Danish winter. In time one of the doors, usually that on the north side, was walled up. Only a few of the Romanesque churches had porches from the outset, but in time porches were nearly always added to the south wall. One of the principal purposes which the porches served was to provide a place where a man could leave his weapons before going in to worship. A medieval church porch was even given the name "våbenhus" or weapon-house.

Few Romanesque churches were built with towers, but in time it became accepted that a parish church should have at least one tower, which could serve as a belfry and a landmark visible for miles, as well as conferring dignity on the building and all it stood for. These towers were, for the most part, Gothic in style, with gable ends both to the east and the west.

The outer walls of these churches were usually left plain, decoration being concentrated in the gables. These were divided by semi-columns or pilaster strips and further decorated by ornamental recesses. As years passed and fashions changed the tendency was to have more recesses, some pointed at the head, some circular, some triangular, some horizontal. There were also more of the so-called corbie stones pointing heavenwards. The variety seems almost unlimited.

From the beginning of the fifteenth century recesses shaped like shields and originally with painted coats of arms, made their appearance. These recesses were often placed obliquely, as shields would appear when worn.

Knowledge of how to design a Romanesque church seems to have been passed on through the towns and villages of Denmark by example rather than by detailed instruction. A painstaking and expert examination of all the Romanesque village churches in the county of Sorø, which number about eighty, has shown that the dimensions of all of them are different. No two churches have ground-plans which fully correspond with each other, yet even to the untutored eye there is a distinctive style in which nearly all Romanesque churches in Denmark were built.

People living in Denmark in medieval times had the privilege of seeing a profusion of brilliant paintings covering the walls whenever they entered their parish church. That visitors to a number of churches today can well imagine how they looked at different periods between the beginning of the twelfth and the middle of the sixteenth century is due to a combination of chance survival, changes in faith and painstaking work of restoration.

In time virtually the whole of the interior walls of the church, including the vaults, came to be covered. Some of the paintings have been continually exposed through the centuries, their original colours growing steadily fainter in consequence. Many were whitewashed over after the Reformation. This was a gradual, not a violent process. Some wall

FRESCOES BY THE ELMELUNDE
MASTER
ELMELUNDE, ISLAND OF MØN

paintings were no doubt removed from view because their message was deemed to be offensive or doctrinally unsound, but evidence suggests that whitewash was applied more frequently because the paintings had become grimy or faded. Removal of the whitewash was the beginning of a process of restoration which in time was to reveal clearly a rich blend of art and faith, naivete and narrative, colour and inspiration.

In many of the early Danish wall paintings Byzantine influence is evident. This is hardly surprising when one considers how much western European art in the early centuries of the second millennium owed to Byzantium. French, German and English influences are also clearly observable, and a number of the painters are known to have been skilled, immigrant craftsmen.

DETAIL
FRESCO
SKIVHOLME CHURCH

FRESCO
SKIVHOLME CHURCH

Nevertheless a distinctively Danish school of wall painting had been established in Zealand, for example, in the twelfth century. In five of the churches, those at Alsted, Broby, Fjenneslev, Forslev and Slaglille, there is a similarity of style, yet expert study shows that they are not the work of the same master.

In one of them, the church at Fjenneslev, a painting on the east wall of the nave shows bearded Magi bearing gifts and hurrying to the scene with movements suggestive of runners in a relay race. Immediately below are contemporary figures of church benefactors, a man holding a model of a church with, behind him, his wife bearing a gold ring.

There is indeed a striking contrast between the Byzantine figures, who for the most part have little individuality, and some of the paintings in which the artists, a number of them certainly indigenous, have clearly drawn on their own imagination and experience.

That biblical scenes should predominate is to be expected, yet there are also numerous representations of ecclesiastical happenings, some of them far from reverent. In Ørslev church, for example, a painting in the south chapel shows four priests with chalices. Somehow one has the feeling that the chalices are rather well filled. Above are some dancers engaged in more or less voluptuous movements. What they are in fact performing is a medieval chain dance, which still survives in the Faroe Islands. The music is being provided by a dog-like animal, who is blowing a trumpet.

With the passage of time, imagination added much. In Ringsted church, for instance, Mary is spectacularly crowned in Heaven with attendant angels. Written text and floral motifs combine to create an exhilarating feeling of circular movement. In Sæby in Jutland the frescoes tell the story of Mary's reputed parents, Anna and Joachim, who were deemed unworthy to have children until Anna learnt, through a form of divine revelation, that she would give birth to the future Virgin Mother.

Changes in architectural fashion, with the advent of the Gothic, led to considerable structural modifications, sometimes to transformation, of

Danish Romanesque churches. In wall paintings, by contrast, it is as easy to find continuity as change over several centuries. As the paintings continued to be produced in the age of High Gothic and even, in some instances, after the Reformation, later developments will be considered in the chapter which follows.

Most of the Danish Viking art which survives is in the form of carving. What may well be considered the earliest artistic masterpiece to be seen in Denmark today, the Bronze Age sun chariot in the National Museum in Copenhagen, is a carved figure. It might therefore be reasonably supposed that the main glories of Denmark's medieval churches would take the form of stone sculpture. In fact, in contrast with Romanesque churches in many other countries, whose exteriors are richly ornamented with stone carvings, some depicting saints, some telling complex narratives, many Danish churches in the same style are strikingly bare on the outside. One explanation of this may be found in the materials available. In Denmark there was, for instance, none of the marble which was used to such spectacular effect in Italian churches. Many of the carvings which do appear on the exteriors of Danish Romanesque churches are, in fact, in the regions where granite is most plentiful.

Viking traditions survive in ashlar carvings on the outside of a number of

MODERN ALTAR IN THE
ANCIENT CATHEDRAL OF RIBE

FRESCO
RÅSTED CHURCH

early Romanesque churches. There are stylised dragons and borders
formed by the coils of snakes. There are lions and lambs, wolves and
pigs, sphinxes and basilisks. Carved on the church at Hansted in Jutland
is a ship with rounded bows and a side rudder. In another Jutland
church a man is depicted with a bird's head.

The human form is a comparative rarity, appearing mostly in hunting
scenes, but there is an abundance of acanthus, rosettes and other forms
of foliage. Expressions of piety are fewer than might be expected,
although on the exterior of one church on the island of Mors the hand
of God is shown blessing the earth.

For Romanesque carving of distinction we have to look rather at the
interiors of churches. Among the greatest creations of this art are a
number of highly decorated altars. The first impression of anyone
seeing them may be of a golden panorama of biblical scenes.

Seven of these so-called golden altars still survive in Denmark. All were
made in Jutland. Five are in the National Museum in Copenhagen. The
others are still in the churches for which they were intended, in Sahl
and Stadil.

The oldest and most richly ornamented, the Lisbjerg altar, was completed
about the middle of the twelfth century. At one time in Lisbjerg church,
it had almost certainly earlier decorated the high altar in Aarhus
cathedral. It is now in the National Museum in Copenhagen. The latest,
probably that in Stadil, dates from about a century later.

The term "golden" is applicable only to the appearance of the altars.
They were in fact made of gilded copper and embossed, that is to say
worked from the back into reliefs. Some details were chased from the
front. Where the altars have been damaged it is easy to see how paper-
thin the metal sheets are, and how surprisingly fragile the whole
structure.

The altars consist of two parts: the frontal, which covers the lower part,
and the retable, which is placed above. A close examination of the frontals
reveals the extraordinary range of subjects treated. No less apparent is the

masterly arrangement of the different, often contrasting figures and the evident determination to fill every available space. The range of dramatis personae in some of them is such that one may even

GOLDEN ALTAR

SAHL CHURCH

DETAIL, GOLDEN ALTAR
SAHL CHURCH

DETAIL, GOLDEN ALTAR
SAHL CHURCH

be tempted to make a comparison with a village nativity play or pageant in which as many people as possible must be given a part.

The central figure is usually Christ, but in one case it is the Virgin Mary, who is surrounded by episodes from her life. Many of the scenes depicted are from the childhood or passion of Christ. But there are also other familiar biblical events, such as the offering of Isaac. There are a number of other Old Testament figures, Moses and Jonah among them, and an interesting variety of saints, supplemented by angels, cherubs and representatives of virtues such as patience and fidelity. In one frontal there is an enactment of the conversion to Christianity of King Harald Bluetooth after the ordeal by fire.

In addition to the various expressions of piety and orthodoxy there are representations of animal figures, which belong to an older, pre-Christian tradition. The animals appear mainly in the decorative bands placed between the main scenes. On one band twelve animals entangled with one another can be seen winding in and out of a figure of eight.

Animals also appear in the interlacements in acanthus scrolls. These include birds of prey, dragons and lions. They all appear ferocious, but in one instance, rather than fight each other, the animals face the same way and bite the backsides of those in front of them.

If space permitted, the artist might fill it with eight-leaved rosettes or tiny crosses. The altars were also originally ornamented with rock crystals, but few of these remain.

The arrangements of the figures in the retables contrast strikingly with those in the frontals. In the retables there is only a single row of figures placed within an architectural framework. The figures are separated by arched columns or small towers. The later the altar the more complex the architectural details become.

Above the retables, surrounded by a Romanesque arch, is a Christ figure. These figures vary considerably according to their date. Some of the crucifixes have clearly been cut to enable them to be put in the space available.

As in much Danish medieval art foreign influences can be discerned in the golden altars. The drapery in the Lisbjerg altar is based on styles to be seen in English sculptures and illuminated manuscripts. French influence is apparent elsewhere. But the artists who made them were employed in Danish workshops, predominantly in the Aarhus area. They were rich in both skills and faith. A Latin text to be seen on one of the altars expresses something of that faith:

"There is one Almighty, not three, and God is one. The very same God distinguishes among various things and

DETAIL, GOLDEN ALTAR
SAHL CHURCH

CHRISTMAS
SAHL CHURCH

DETAIL, VENG CHURCH FONT

controls everything. Whatever is, whatever is alive, whatever is moving, I make alive, move, provide for and support, including the external as well as penetrating the innermost matters. Under all matters and over all matters I move everything. God is eternal."

The most abundant stone carvings to be found in the interiors of Danish Romanesque churches are the fonts. They number about two thousand in all, some in sandstone, the majority in granite. They were large enough to allow total immersion during baptism.

The fonts were painted black with designs in bright colours. They were originally placed near the entrance to the church, but after the Reformation they

GRANITE LION FONT
VENG CHURCH

were moved to permit the congregation in their pews to have a clear view of altar and pulpit as well as the font.

In Veng church in Jutland there is an exceptionally fine font dating from the twelfth century, with a human head placed on a double-bodied lion. The lion's tail, which symbolised strength, was once brightly gilded, but, as on other fonts and, indeed, on early Danish carvings generally, this has been wholly lost.

In Romanesque churches in other countries, France for example, lions can be seen in the peripheral decorations. In Denmark they are often a principal feature. Some of the designs have a complexity suggestive of Viking style. There are altogether some two hundred lion fonts in Denmark, more than are to be found in any other country.

There is an abundance of wood carving in the Romanesque churches, with crucifixes understandably predominating. In the early works the arms of the crucifix and, in some instances, Christ's hands were attached to the larger pieces of wood with glue, nails or pegs. An interesting variant of this technique is to be found in Sorø church, where the Christ figure is carved in relief out of the cross itself. In a number of churches, for example in Ørslev, the cross is shaped in such a way as to suggest that it is also the tree of life.

FONT MADE OF RED MARBLE OBTAINED FROM GOTLAND. THE ONLY DANISH FONT WHICH ALWAYS CONTAINS WATER. BECAUSE OF THE MARBLE THE WATER REMAINS FRESH

GRØNBAEK CHURCH

With such relatively primitive techniques crucifixes were created which a sensitive viewer must surely find deeply moving.

One such is the Åby crucifix, now in the National Museum in Copenhagen. The being depicted here can be seen as an embodiment of the transition from Viking custom to Christian faith, from warrior king to the Christ who died that others might live. The Åby Christ is a royal figure, a conqueror even on the cross. His hair and moustache are Viking style, and the symbols of his status are a crown and a necklace. He is far removed from the suffering Christ of so much great European art, but he has a haunting quality of his own.

DETAIL OF ÅBY CRUCIFIX

An exact replica of the Åby crucifix is to be seen in the crypt of the church of Our Lady in Aarhus, a more rewarding setting than any museum can provide. Massive stone Romanesque arches are lit only by two candles. The crucifix stands alone, a Christ-captain, with the background of a cross, who could surely have sailed to Byzantium and beyond.

In stained glass, one of the glories of medieval churches in a number of European countries, Denmark is not rich. By contrast there are some beautiful early ivory pieces now housed in museums. Among the most interesting are a Sicilian cross in elephant ivory of Byzantine inspiration and the seal of Roskilde cathedral in narwhal tusk.

Another intriguing piece has a drawing
in Anglo-Saxon style and a runic
inscription.

Of exceptional interest are the so-called
aquamaniles. These were water-carriers
in the form of a horse and rider which
were used by priests for the ritual
washing of hands during mass and
known as aquamanile. In these beautiful
small bronze objects it is perhaps possible
to see a symbol, the figure of a Danish
horseman riding confidently towards a
future of greatness.

Before that future could be attained
immense difficulties had to be overcome.

DETAIL

AQUAMANILE, SMALL
MEDIEVAL WATER RECEPTACLE
NATIONAL MUSEUM,
COPENHAGEN

III.

THE GOTHIC AGE

*""The main voice of Denmark goes withal" –
Laertes, Hamlet*

**ALTAR BY CLAUS BERG
DETAIL: MARY AND CHILD
ODENSE CATHEDRAL**

By the middle of the fourteenth century
the Gothic style was firmly established in
Denmark.

The great Danish cathedrals are
predominantly Gothic in design. A clear
exception is Ribe, where the building of
a Romanesque cathedral was begun in
the middle of the twelfth century and
continued for about a hundred years. It is
in the form of a basilica, with a nave
flanked by two aisles on either side. As
such it is unique among Danish
churches, as is the great dome over
twenty-one metres high. All this
combines to create an impressive sense of
spaciousness and light. Two towers of
equal height were constructed on the
west side, but on Christmas night in
1283 one of them collapsed, killing a
number of people. It was later replaced
by a brick tower.

Ribe's cathedral was built of volcanic tufa imported from the Rhineland. In Viborg it was decided to build a massive church in granite. Over the centuries the church suffered from fires and neglect, and it was reconstructed in its present form in the 1860s and 1870s. As an attempt to recreate, both in materials and atmosphere, a Romanesque cathedral it is likely to have a powerful impact on anyone who visits it, but, apart from its crypt, it is in reality a form of nineteenth century architecture and will later in this work be considered as such.

In other cities cathedrals were preceded by earlier church structures, which were then demolished to allow a new building in Gothic style to be erected. In Roskilde, for instance, a wooden church was replaced by two stone churches –one of them donated by the widow of a man

ALTAR BY CLAUS BERG
DETAIL: QUEEN CHRISTINE,
QUEEN ELISABETH AND
ELISABETH OF
BRANDENBURG
ODENSE CATHEDRAL

murdered on the orders of Knud the Great – before the present brick structure was begun in the late twelfth century.

Roskilde cathedral is not the oldest brick church in Denmark. This distinction is claimed for St Bendt's church in Ringsted, another monument to a murdered man. The victim in this instance was Duke Knud Lavard, father of King Valdemar I. (Valdemar was born a week after his father's death.) The murdered man was canonised at a solemn ceremony in Ringsted in 1170, shortly after the building of the church was begun. But Roskilde's ecclesiastical prestige was such that where it led other cities were likely to follow.

In the new Roskilde cathedral two storeys had been constructed, including a gallery and a south transept, when all building was stopped and plans were changed. This decision was evidently made by Peder Sunesen, who had succeeded the great Absalon as bishop. Sunesen, like Absalon, had studied at the St Geneviève monastery in Paris and had been much impressed by the new chapel added to Tournai cathedral. This was built above an arch over the road which connected the cathedral with the bishop's palace. A similar design was adopted for Roskilde.

The shape of the cathedral is an aisled basilica with a triforium, that is to say a gallery above the arches. The external walls stand on granite ashlars. The oldest bricks are all red, but some of the later ones are wholly yellow, others mottled. The vaults were constructed over a period of some two hundred years, styles ranging from Romanesque to late Gothic. Fifteenth century additions include a porch and a beautiful, small vestibule believed to have been brought from a town on the German Baltic coast.

One of the chapels built in the same century served to give Roskilde its unique place in the history and traditions of the Danish royal family. Known as the Chapel of the Magi, it was created for a new brotherhood of the Holy Trinity founded by King Christian I in 1462. This, it was decided, was to be the burial place of King Christian, his queen and their sons. A tradition of royal burials in Roskilde was thereby established which would bring about the extraordinary range of architectural styles, characteristic of several centuries, which immediately impresses the visitor to Roskilde cathedral today.

A curious feature of the chapel of the Magi is a central column of polished granite, having a base with palmettes in Romanesque style. It was fashioned in the late twelfth century. Marks on it indicate the height of Danish kings and other royal personages through the centuries. How accurate these are is questionable, for the highest mark, at 219 centimetres, is significantly that of the chapel's founder, Christian I, whose skeleton is some thirty centimetres shorter. Among those accorded marks on the column were Tsar Alexander III of Russia and the exiled King Michael of Romania. Low down on the column comes the mark of King Edward VIII of England, better known as the Duke of Windsor.

Another adornment of the cathedral of considerable historic interest is the sarcophagus of Queen Margrethe, the

CHAPEL OF THE MAGI
ROSKILDE CATHEDRAL

SARCOPHAGUS OF CROWN
PRINCE CHRISTIAN, SON OF
CHRISTIAN IV, WHO DIED
BEFORE HIS FATHER
ROSKILDE CATHEDRAL

effective founder of the Kalmar Union of the three Scandinavian countries in 1397. She herself had expressed a wish to be buried, as her father and grandfather had been, in Sorø, but the Bishop of Roskilde intervened forcefully. The funeral took place in Roskilde, and a tomb with an alabaster effigy was placed in front of the high altar of the cathedral in 1423. It is an impressive work, showing the Queen as a young woman with bells on her dress. It was almost certainly made in Lübeck.

Like that in Roskilde the cathedral in Odense, though Gothic in design, has origins going back to the earlier years of Christianity in Denmark. A wooden church had been built and dedicated to St Alban. Here in 1086 King Knud II, when kneeling before the altar, was murdered together with his bodyguard. Knud was later canonised, and Odense, lavishly provided with monasteries and convents, became a place of pilgrimage.

The adoption of the Gothic style to supersede an earlier stone church began at the end of the thirteenth century. The work of construction, culminating in a brick building, with buttresses, pointed arch, ribbed vaulting and a large nave and chancel, took some two hundred years to complete. The first impression the visitor is likely to have is of spaciousness, light and whitewashed walls, but eyes will soon be drawn to the altar. This is a glorious triptych, nearly five metres high. There are some three hundred carved figures and an abundance of gold. The main theme is the Crucifixion, but apostles, St Francis of Assisi and members of the Danish royal family are among those portrayed.

The sculptor was Claus Berg of Lübeck, who set up a workshop in Odense and created other altars and crucifixes in Denmark. Outstanding among them is the huge crucifix in Sorø church. His central panel in Odense cathedral may be based on a work by Lucas Cranach, the great German painter in the service of the Elector of Saxony. Claus Berg's style has been described, colourfully and appropriately, as Baroque Gothic.

Aarhus cathedral, which is the longest ecclesiastical building in Denmark, began as a Romanesque structure with three massive arches over the nave. Extensive damage was caused by fire, reconstruction in Gothic style beginning in the fourteenth century. A major change occurred when both chancel and side-aisles were extended, the feeling

BERNT NOTKE

DETAIL, PAINTING OF BISHOP

JENS LANGE

AARHUS CATHEDRAL

of space being enhanced by a large ambulatory of a kind uncommon in Denmark.

Anyone who walks around the ambulatory or studies other walls in this massive cathedral must surely be impressed, and intrigued, by some of the fresco paintings. One is a pictorial

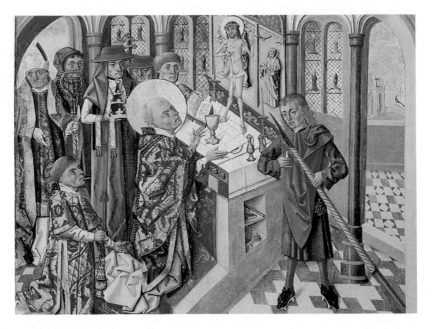

PAINTING BY BERNT NOTKE

AARHUS CATHEDRAL

narrative in which those who take part include the Devil at work and Aarhus citizens dressed in fifteenth century costumes.

The painting is on three levels. At the bottom purgatory is depicted with some rather nasty tortures inflicted on sinners, though hope is offered by angels transporting the souls of the blessed to Heaven. On the top tier the Holy Trinity sit surrounded by angelic musicians.

Between Heaven and Hell well-to-do citizens line up in front of an altar to receive the eucharist and thereby, it is implied, advance to the upper rather than the lower tier. Some of these citizens are youthful, evidently interested in fashion and, it may be supposed, exchanging the gossip of the day.

An even more immediately impressive, because more colourfully restored, fresco painting shows St George in the act of slaying the dragon. He has clearly just emerged from a castle, but for the rest the background is suggestive of tapestry.

Like that in Odense the cathedral in Aarhus has a magnificent altar, the creation of another Lübeck sculptor, Bernt Notke. A startling feature of this is a spire rising above the altar, on top of which Christ stands crucified.

During recent restoration work a number of paintings were discovered on the back of the altar-piece. In one of these St Christopher is shown carrying the infant Jesus on his shoulder. Another saint featured is, understandably, St Clement, deemed by many to be the patron saint of seamen. For centuries sailors, making for Aarhus harbour, have been able to see Aarhus cathedral towering in front of them.

The number of cathedral cities in Denmark is comparatively small. The few there are have been richly endowed with ecclesiastical buildings since medieval times. In a number of them work of distinction in Gothic style is to be seen.

As well as the cathedral, Odense has an ancient abbey church dedicated to St Hans. This church has a long chancel in Gothic style which was added in the middle of the fifteenth century. There is

DETAILS
PAINTING BY BERNT NOTKE
AARHUS CATHEDRAL

also a structure believed to be unique in Denmark, which was erected in the southern aisle. From the inside it is reached by steps. From the outside what is thought to be a pulpit can be seen through an arch. This pulpit, supposedly, was used for preaching to lepers.

In the design and ornamentation of Denmark's Gothic cathedrals foreign influence is evident. This is not in itself surprising. As a sea-going nation, dependent on trade and importing much, Danes have consistently enriched their culture with the arts and styles of other people.

Denmark has also served as a channel for cultural imports into Scandinavia as a whole. This largely classicising effect has caused a distinguished Danish medievalist to describe Denmark as being in some respects the Italy of Scandinavia. Shakespeare indeed made Horatio describe himself as "more an antique Roman than a Dane."

In the fourteenth century, however, two events occurred which profoundly influenced Danish arts and crafts for centuries to come and transformed the relationship between the indigenous and the imported. One was an affliction for which there was at the time no known remedy. The other was an exceptionally skilful exploitation of commercial and political power.

The affliction was the bubonic plague, which reached Europe in 1347, transmitted, it was thought, in Genoese ships sailing from the Black Sea. The Black Death, as it was called, reached Denmark in 1349 and is estimated to have killed a quarter of the population. The Black Death was devastating wherever it struck, not only through loss of life, but in the general demoralisation and hysteria it engendered. But its effects were probably greatest in northern countries with their small populations and relatively hard living conditions. In southern Europe the plague even served as a source of inspiration, as the danse macabre and sculpted figures in shrouds on tombs made clear.

The commercial and political exploitation was by the Hanseatic League, which by the end of the fourteenth century had become arguably the most powerful force in northern Europe. Originally formed by groups of merchants to protect their trading interests, it developed into an association of seventy major towns, mostly in Germany, and about a hundred lesser ones, with Lübeck generally having the most powerful voice. The League controlled the export trade of the Nordic countries in grain, furs, timber and, to some extent, fish as well as the imports of a number of manufactured goods, such as textiles. It imposed trade embargoes, its

TOMB OF QUEEN
MARGARETHE I
ROSKILDE CATHEDRAL

fleet at times controlled the Sound, and its representatives tended to dominate the councils of a number of Scandinavian cities.

In 1370 the province of Scania, until then under Danish rule, was ceded to the Hanseatic League for fifteen years. Later the whole of the island of Bornholm was mortgaged to Lübeck for half a century. Some impression of the relative prosperity of Danish rulers and Hanseatic merchants can be had from a letter written by Margrethe, later to be Queen of Norway and Sweden as well as Denmark. The letter was addressed to her husband, the King of Norway, and she went on to beg him to ask a German merchant to send her certain provisions and to promise to pay for them later.

The almost inevitable consequence of all this was a kind of cultural colonisation by North Germans. German universities served as magnets, German artists practised in Denmark, and Danish artists went to Germany for their training. Hence the vestibule in Roskilde cathedral. Hence too the sarcophagus for the body of Queen Margrethe made in Lübeck, and the cathedral altars in Odense and Aarhus.

The change from indigenous to German-dominated art was neither immediate nor total. In wall paintings there was, as has been stated earlier, evident continuity. Indeed distinctive qualities in Danish architecture served to foster this. Danish Gothic churches have few of the huge windows characteristic of the style in a number of other countries. In consequence there was plenty of space for painting on walls as well as vaults and columns, and advantage was taken of the opportunities.

A startling example of how this was done is to be seen in a church in Dronninglund. Here eight figures from a cosmopolitan past are seen engaged in four chivalrous combats. The Trojan Hector fights King David, Charlemagne fights Joshua, and Godfrey of Bouillon fights Judas Maccabeus. The strangest encounter of all is between Alexander of Macedon and Arthur of Britain. Alexander is riding an elephant and Arthur a camel. The choice of a camel seems a strange one.

Rich variety is to be seen in the work of some of the artists. In Kirkerup, for instance, there are three adjacent paintings. On the top left there are naked temptresses who are indeed tempting. To the right a scene from the Day of Judgment shows some small devils, malevolent, no doubt, yet rather attractive. Below are scenes from Noah's ark, those on board including a pleasantly domesticated man and wife, some slightly quarrelsome birds and some evidently contented fish.

Satirical and irreverent treatment of familiar themes is more pungent and more widespread than in the Romanesque frescoes. One artist left his permanent imprint on two churches in Jutland, those in Sæby and Vrå, by painting the same picture on their walls. This shows a horrifying devil removing the soul of a man who has just died while his widow, a pretty, slightly demure creature, is clearly enjoying the attentions of a handsome young lover. Elsewhere in Sæby church is a painting of the Last Judgment, in which a pope and a bishop

**CLAUS BERG ALTAR DETAIL
CHURCH OF OUR LADY
AARHUS**

**CLAUS BERG ALTAR
CHURCH OF OUR LADY
AARHUS**

are on their way to Hell. In Vrå the artist has included a pig playing the lute among biblical scenes.

Other painters too imposed their personalities on church walls. We cannot be certain of their nationality, but their styles are distinctly Danish. One of these signed his name as "Martinus Maler" or Martin the Painter on the walls of more than one church in Zealand. In Gimlinge he portrayed acrobatic attempts by souls to tilt the balance of the scales which were to decide their fate in the after-life. In his painting in Gerlev church the provisions at the Last Supper consist of medieval Danish dishes.

CARVINGS FROM
CHOIR STALLS
ROSKILDE CATHEDRAL

Another prolific painter of the late fifteenth and early sixteenth centuries is known as the Elmelunde Master. His

work is to be seen in a number of churches on the island of Møn and the neighbouring mainland. His figures are somewhat crude and have been compared by a Danish historian with woodcuts in a poor man's bible. But such is the profusion of his paintings on the walls and vaulting of the church in Keldby, for example, that he has created the impression of an enchanted bower. Events in Danish history are also commemorated on church walls. In St Peter's church in Næstved there is a memorial picture of King Valdemar Atterdag and his Queen Helvig, which was painted shortly after the King's death in 1375. In two Zealand churches, in Højby and Skamstrup, the sailing race between St Olav and his brother Harald, for which the prize was the crown of Norway, is depicted.

This tradition was maintained up to the time of the Reformation. A wall painting in the church at Snoldelev, not far from Copenhagen, is copied from a woodcut on the title page of King Christian III's bible. This was the first bible to be translated into Danish. The painting dates from the second half of the sixteenth century.

Such is the wealth of well preserved or well restored wall paintings executed over four and a half centuries that a carefully planned tour of early Danish churches can be a richly rewarding experience.

DETAILS, CHOIR STALLS
ROSKILDE CATHEDRAL

Much of the finest Gothic art in Denmark was created with the use of wood, either through carving or as a surface for painting. Many of the paintings are on the wings of altar-pieces, whose central panels are carved. These panels would be left open or closed according to whether or not the painting was deemed appropriate to a particular festival, saint's day or season.

A number of the altar-pieces were imported, some from Lübeck, others from Danzig. The paintings are rich in colour; blue, red and green supplementing the dominant gold. Gilt surfaces were given punched patterns, and a number of precious stones, rock crystal and turquoise in particular, were inserted.

Many of the finest carvings were of crucifixes. If a single fourteenth century crucifix is to be singled out for repeated viewing and perpetual wonder, it may perhaps be the Skovlænge church masterpiece, which is now to be seen in the Maribo museum. This is a representation of a truly suffering Christ, with skin like parchment and torn hands. His head is bowed, there are blood-clots on his arms, and his exceptionally long legs serve to increase the prevailing sense of melancholy.

Another masterpiece of carving in wood is the narrative told in the choir of Roskilde cathedral. Whereas the chapels in the cathedral provide a kind of brief pictorial history of Denmark, the Gothic carvings above the choir stalls serve as a journey through the bible and beyond. The Creation is followed by such highlights as the murder of Abel by Cain, Jews worshipping the golden calf and Jonah spewed out of the whale's mouth. The culmination is the crowning of the Virgin Mary and Doomsday.

Many churches in Denmark are adorned by ships' models, for the most part suspended from ceilings. This is in no way surprising. Through the centuries not a few of Denmark's countless seafarers vowed that if their prayers were answered, and they reached harbour safely, they would make an appropriate gift to their local church. These models, many of them of exquisite workmanship, number over a thousand and date from around 1600.

A particularly fine one of some historic
interest is to be seen in Ebeltoft church.
It and a painting represent a warship
named Maria, which formed part of the
fleet in which Christian II sailed to
Sweden, an enterprise that led to the
perpetration of the so-called Stockholm
bloodbath, in which some of the most
powerful men in Sweden were executed.
When in exile later, and in need of
money, Christian sold the Maria to an
Italian, who had her converted into a
merchant vessel operating in the
Mediterranean. The ship's model was
made in 1521, the year after the
Stockholm bloodbath.

BERNT NOTKE ALTAR DETAIL
AARHUS CATHEDRAL

In 1429 the goldsmiths of Copenhagen
received their first charter, which
included regulations for ensuring high
standards of workmanship and quality of
metal. This was a formal recognition of a
craft, which, like that of the silversmiths,
had been practised for centuries, not only
in the main centres of population, but in
small provincial towns. Bishop Absalon's
will, for instance, dating from 1201,
includes an imposing list of silver bowls,
beakers and plates.

BERNT NOTKE ALTAR DETAIL
AARHUS CATHEDRAL

Much fine work in both metals was lost
in a country where from time to time
over the centuries even kings and other
powerful magnates were desperately
short of funds and obliged to sell valued
possessions. Another reason for the loss
of fine works of art was the regrettable
practice of using old silver to make new

objects. When one considers that many of the cathedrals and larger churches had fifty altars or more, for each of which liturgical vessels were provided, the scale of the loss is seen to be lamentable.

Some of the best works in gold and silver which have survived from the time when Gothic styles were fashionable either received special protection by churches or emerged from latter-day excavations. Among these is a beautifully rounded gold chalice, which was presented to Roskilde cathedral at the time of Queen Margrethe's funeral for the benefit of her soul. The upper surface of the foot shows a crucifix and the Danish national coat of arms.

The chalice is now in the National Museum in Copenhagen. No less impressive, and in the same museum, is the Queen Margrethe beaker made of silver and vertically fluted. Each of the eight flutes has a vertical band. The belt is ornamented with leaves.

Among the finds of gold and jewellery was one from Clausholm in Jutland dating from the first half of the fourteenth century. This included a ring clasp consisting of six lilies in filigree, interspersed with pearls and garnets. It too is in the National Museum in Copenhagen, as are some exquisite brooches of gold, turquoise and amethysts discovered near Viborg.

Dredging operations in Randers fjord brought to light, among other treasures, a walrus ivory chess piece, showing a queen, who is on horseback and accompanied by two men and two women. The men are armed and the women presumably ladies-in-waiting. One of the finest pieces of ivory dating from the early thirteenth century is a crucifix from the Benedictine monastery in Herlufsholm, in which the bowed head of Christ and his loincloth seem to be in perpetual haunting motion.

CROWN OF THORNS, ALTAR
LØYT CHURCH

Virtually all the artistic treasures created between the coming of Christianity to Denmark and the Reformation which still survive were executed as expressions of faith or, for other reasons, in the service of the Church. Even in architecture surprisingly little secular work in Gothic style is to be seen today. An interesting exception is Gørslev castle in Zealand, whose main wing was built about 1400. (Even this is in the form of a cross.) Its dominant feature is a tower some thirty metres high of a kind rarely encountered elsewhere.

GETHSAMANE, ALTAR
LØYT CHURCH

With the discovery of Renaissance arts in other countries of Europe new sources of inspiration would be found. But decades would still pass before the consequences of the Black Death and the Hanseatic stranglehold were altogether overcome.

THE RESURRECTION, ALTAR
LØYT CHURCH

IV.

THE COMING OF THE RENAISSANCE

SCEPTRE: GOLD WITH ENAMEL
AND TABLE-CUT DIAMONDS
ROSENBORG, COPENHAGEN

"That fair and war-like form in which the majesty of buried Denmark did sometimes march" – Horatio, Hamlet

Anyone who wants to see examples of Viking art in Denmark today must go to a museum. Romanesque and Gothic art is virtually all church art. The arts of the Renaissance are more widespread, but much that is best and most characteristic of them is to be found in a number of castles.

There is also a wealth of domestic architecture of the same period. Many of the houses have been restored, or even reconstructed, but in general their appeal to the eye has not suffered in consequence. Indeed in a number of the houses it may have been significantly enhanced.

The Renaissance castles were built or rebuilt on the orders of one monarch, Christian IV, who came to the throne in 1588 and reigned for sixty years. During

this time he reconstructed Hamlet's castle of Elsinore, left an abiding mark as a city planner of Copenhagen, took a particular delight in the palace built for him in a park a little outside the capital, and created the building which today houses the Museum of the National History of Denmark.

Christian IV was not widely travelled, but as a fluent Latin speaker, a lover of music, a student of mathematics and one whose principal delight, apart from women, was in beautiful buildings, he looked southward, beyond the Baltic, for the artists and craftsmen he needed.

As a patron he had an immense advantage over his predecessors. The Reformation came peacefully to Denmark, and a Lutheran state church was well established by the middle of the

SWORD OF PRINCE ELECT
THE SWORD HILT IS FORMED
OF THREE SNAKES, EACH
BITING A HEART. GOLD,
ENAMEL AND DIAMONDS. THE
SNAKES SYMBOLISE WISDOM
AND THE HEARTS COURAGE
ROSENBORG, COPENHAGEN

LEGENDARY HERO
HOLGER DANSKE
KRONBORG

sixteenth century. As part of the settlement the property of bishops and monasteries was transferred to the Crown. With this, and large sums received annually from the dues paid by the owners of ships passing through the Sound, Christian IV was able to indulge his tastes.

A number of those whom he brought to Denmark to work for him came from the Low Countries, among them being the gifted Steenwinckel family from Antwerp. The work they did and the examples they set largely decided the nature of Danish Renaissance architecture.

Theirs was a style which served spectacularly to express civic pride and mercantile wealth in the great city halls of the Low Countries. It was a form of mannerism, generally known as Dutch Renaissance. It was characterised by high, multi-storeyed, curving gables, often with scrolls on the sides.

The principal materials used in Dutch Renaissance buildings in Denmark are brick and sandstone. The exteriors tend to be severe, the eye being drawn from them to towers of contrasting shapes and differing heights.

Helsingør, which Shakespeare transcribed as Elsinore, was a natural site for a fortress, dominating the Sound as it does. It was also a thriving port regularly visited by English actors, musicians and clowns. After the old castle, the setting for Hamlet, was destroyed by warfare in the sixteenth century, Christian IV's predecessor, Frederik II, had a new castle built which would overlook the Sound.

The site chosen was Kronborg, below which the legendary hero Holger Danske, who would rise to save Denmark when the country was in peril, was believed to sleep. The castle was in Renaissance style, having a large central courtyard with four wings. It was roofed with copper, which gave it, like a number of buildings in Copenhagen, the green tint to be seen today.

The new castle was badly damaged by fire, and the reconstruction ordered by Christian IV created a successful blend of two Dutch Renaissance styles, with due deference paid to the classical originals from which the European Renaissance was derived. The inner courtyard is seen through a rounded archway with Ionic columns on each side, one holding a statue of Neptune in a niche, the other one of Mercury. The chapel, with elaborately carved bench ends and a balcony for the royal family, remains largely as it was after the initial building, though an impressive organ was added with the reconstruction.

FREDERIKSBORG

More revealing of the tastes and style imposed by Christian IV, and a much more ambitious project in itself, is

Frederiksborg Castle. It was built on three small islands and today dominates the town of Hillerød. Hillerød was Christian's birthplace, and he determined to create here a monument by which he would always be remembered,

The castle gives the impression of rising directly out of lakes. The walls are of red brick, above a granite base, and are decorated by horizontal sandstone bands. Octagonal towers are surmounted by spires several storeys high. Although this and the gables are characteristic of Dutch Renaissance architecture, there is some evidence that the Steenwinckel family, who worked on the project under the close supervision of the King, had been influenced by French architectural manuals.

One of the first objects to strike the eye is a large bronze fountain. It is in fact a copy of one originally created by the Florence-trained Dutch sculptor Adriaen de Vries, which was looted by Swedish troops. A figure towering above the rest of the structure is that of Neptune. Other figures represent the fertility of the Danish soil and the Sound and the two Belts.

The planets, with Apollo and Diana representing the sun and the moon, feature prominently in the statuary, for Christian was a firm believer in astrology. The main doorway is in the form of a triumphal arch, adorned with goddesses, palms and laurel leaves. It was erected shortly after Christian's successful campaign against the Swedes in 1611.

In 1859 the interior of Frederiksborg Castle was largely destroyed by fire. Reconstruction was carried out as a gift to the nation by the Carlsberg Foundation, and the castle was transformed into a museum. As such it offers an absorbing tour through much of the history of Denmark during the last century, largely in the form of portraits.

How Christian IV would have viewed these portraits is a subject for speculation. He might well have wondered whether some of the meticulous representations of worthy citizens in sober suits, collars and ties had much relation to art. But his eyes would surely have lit up on seeing the force, indeed savagery, of work done under German occupation in the 1940s and the wit and originality shown in some of the later portraits.

PIETER ISAACSZ
PAINTING OF CHRISTIAN IV
ROSENBORG, COPENHAGEN

Rosenborg Castle was not conceived in the spirit of grandeur which is so evident in Frederiksborg. Christian envisaged it as a retreat from the cramped conditions of Copenhagen and called it at first his summer-house. It was originally created as a modest two-storey building with a turret containing a stairway and topped by a spire. Reconstruction followed within a decade. Additions included the dominant great tower and a long hall, whose decorations had as themes the seven ages of man, the seven planets and the seven liberal arts. Christian now called it his "great house in the garden." The addition of a moat and a drawbridge even offered a playful suggestion of a fortification.

Like Frederiksborg, Rosenborg is today a museum. In contrast with the earlier prevailing fashion of dividing rooms in museums according to the type of object displayed, progress, it was decided, would be in chronological order. As a result the visitor to Rosenborg today has an immediate insight into the life-style of Christian IV as well as into various aspects of Danish Renaissance art, both imported and indigenous.

The first room to be seen is Christian's so-called winter room with panels imported from Antwerp and a ceiling painted with mythological scenes by the Netherlands artist Pieter Isaacsz. Exhibits include a goblet depicting Christian as a young knight made by a Brunswick

ROSENBORG

goldsmith and a bust of him modelled by a Copenhagen sculptor.

In the next room, which was Christian's writing closet, the ceiling paintings show scenes from the Italian epic, Orlando Furioso. Exhibits include a silver lantern made in Copenhagen and a silver mug made in Odense. The Book of Psalms is bound in silver with King David shown playing the harp. There are two bedside lamps of silver and rock crystal depicting ships and an ivory tankard belonging to Christian's daughter Hedevig.

Perhaps the most striking object in the King's bedroom is a table inlaid with silver and mother-of-pearl, on which are placed silver plates engraved with depictions of love scenes and allegories.

This progressive representation of an extraordinary reign is brought to an end with a painting by a Netherlands artist of Christian IV on his death-bed. Visitors continue their spectacular journey by entering the world of the baroque.

Christian IV was an enthusiastic town planner, and the consequences of some of his proposals are to be seen in Copenhagen today, though they are not so immediately apparent as in the more isolated structures of Frederiksborg and Kronborg.

The most ambitious of his proposals for Copenhagen was the creation of a great

STANDING CUP AND COVER
GOLD, ENAMEL, SET WITH
CAMEOS AND INTAGLIOS OF
ANCIENT GODS,
EMPERORS AND OF
EUROPEAN RULERS
ROSENBORG, COPENHAGEN

DETAIL

octagon, of which Rosenborg would form part. As such it did not come into being, but the concept was adopted later to provide the admirable setting in which the Amalienborg Palace is to be seen today.

Among the surviving buildings in Copenhagen on which in one way or another Christian left his imprint are the Stock Exchange and two churches. Deciding that a simple trading hall, with a packing-room in the basement and a few offices on an upper floor, was unworthy of the country over which he reigned, Christian commissioned Ludvig Heidtrider, who was best known as a designer of fireworks, to create a new commercial centre. The outcome was the building dominating a waterfront which can still be seen today, with richly ornamented gables and an almost Gothic, so-called dragon spire.

One of the Renaissance churches served Copenhagen University, the other the Danish Royal Navy. Trinity Church was a parish church, which housed in its attic the University library. Its reconstruction in Renaissance style with Gothic influences, was carried out in conjunction with the building of a round tower and an observatory. The exterior of the round tower consists of alternating red and yellow bricks. Inside is a spiral ramp, more than 200 metres in length, which could be negotiated on horseback or by coach and was used to transport heavy astronomical instruments.

Holmens, the naval church, was built alongside a canal. It is cruciform in shape, with elaborate Renaissance gables. More happily than most other structures built in Copenhagen before the eighteenth century it has been spared the ravages of time, fire and bombardment.

Another Copenhagen building in Dutch Renaissance style which has survived well is to be seen in one of the busiest shopping streets, the Amagertorv. A former merchant's house, it has a richly decorated facade and gables. The interior, which has been wholly reconstructed, today houses products of the Royal Copenhagen Porcelain factory.

Among the other legacies of Christian IV to be seen in Copenhagen today is the copper and gilt Caritas fountain, which shows a pregnant young woman with a child in her arms and a boy at her side. A number of dolphins are in attendance.

Christian's influence and that of the Dutch, is also to be seen in the district known as Christianshavn. In the sixteenth century Christian II had induced a number of Dutch families, whose skills as market gardeners he admired, to settle on the island of Amager, where Copenhagen airport now stands. When Christian IV decided to build a new township there he both adopted Dutch plans and used Dutch labour. As in a number of Dutch cities canals were an essential feature of the enterprise.

Christian's legacies apart, some of the outstanding architectural achievements of the Danish Renaissance are to be seen in manor houses in the country and rich merchants' town houses.

ARTIST UNKNOWN
JACOB ULFELDT, DANISH
AMBASSADOR TO THE
NETHERLANDS, AND HIS
FAMILY
FREDERIKSBORG

DETAIL

JENS BANG'S HOUSE
AALBORG

ROUND TOWER
COPENHAGEN

The most spectacular of the manor houses retain something of the quality of earlier fortified castles. A striking example is Rosenholm in Jutland, which has been occupied by the Rosenkrantz family – "come Rosencrantz and gentle Guildenstern" – for well over four hundred years. It has four wings with towers and spires and a pavilion in the grounds which served as a kind of private university. As at Frederiksborg advantage has been taken of the flatness of the Danish countryside and the abundance of water, so that, through the construction of moats, Rosenholm gives the impression of rising out of a lake.

Another example of spectacular use of water is the manor house of Søbygård near Marstal in Fyn. Here a small lake was formed by damming a stream. On islands with high sides made with granite boulders, and connected by drawbridges, a castle-like building and a three-winged farmhouse were constructed.

Arguably the most splendid of the merchants' houses in Renaissance style was that of Jens Bang of Aalborg, who in

the 1620s had a mansion constructed of brick and sandstone, with three large gables lavishly ornamented. In a number of Danish towns buildings have been created, or recreated, with meticulous care and at no small expense which enable the inhabitants, and visitors, to picture the homes in which, centuries ago, well-to-do Danes dwelt and traded, created and worshipped.

The centre of Ribe, for example, has been most successfully maintained as an area of narrow, winding, cobbled streets and half-timbered houses. In Aarhus the area known as Den Gamle By (or Old Town) is in effect an open-air museum consisting of some seventy houses transported from various parts of Denmark, reassembled and fitted with furniture and equipment appropriate to the ages of the houses.

So extensive, and intensive, has been the preservation and reconstruction that today the half-timbered house of the seventeenth century is as characteristic of the Danish townscape as is the Romanesque church with whitewashed exterior and Gothic gables of the Danish landscape.

The impact on the eye is particularly pleasing in towns where large numbers of houses have been successfully preserved in and around the central square. One such is Køge, which has a wealth of half-timbered houses, some dating from the late sixteenth century,

ENAMELLED GOLD MEDAL
WITH THE PORTRAIT OF
FREDERIK II

some from the seventeenth. Most are painted a rich yellow on a brick or stone surface. They tend to be single-storeyed, with steeply sloping roofs, giving them a slightly squat appearance.

A number of Køge's early houses have inner courtyards, some with shops, for example a hairdresser's or a greengrocer's. In a few the trade practised is indicated by a distinctive sign. A twisted chimney, for instance, traditionally announced the owner to be a blacksmith. One of the most exquisite courtyards, with several half-timbered buildings, for centuries housed a tannery.

Other courtyards now have carefully tended gardens. The owners of most of them have adopted the engaging custom of leaving the outer door open as an indication that, however private the gardens may seem, visitors are welcome to enter them.

Holbæk is another town rich in half-timbered houses, one of which was moved from a position near the harbour to the principal and unusually wide main street. Here it serves as a museum, in which old living rooms and shops have been recreated and silver and pottery are displayed.

In other Danish towns there are a number of whitewashed houses similar in style to those associated with Shakespeare's birthplace, Stratford-on-Avon, and known in England as Elizabethan, though dating for the most part from the middle to the late seventeenth century.

In Danish churches the Reformation brought changes in style for both economic and theological reasons. After the sequestration of funds church building was virtually brought to a halt. The whitewashing of walls removed from view representations of saints and the Virgin Mary as well as some robust, bucolic figures of Danish medieval imagination. But artistically there were gains as well as losses.

One development was a variation of the familiar type of triptych with a centrepiece and movable wings. In the centrepiece the crucifixion could still be portrayed sometimes surmounted by triangular gables, but in the wings, instead of human figures, there were painted words, usually taken from Luther's catechism. The words have continued to serve as a

decoration no less than as a message.
Among a number of such examples of
this new artistic style to be seen in
Jutland churches is an impressive reredos
placed on a Romanesque altar in
Sejerslev.

In Lutheran church services the sermon
played an increasingly important part,
and new provision was made both for
preacher and congregation. Some of the
most splendid pulpits to be seen in
Danish churches today are Renaissance
creations. One such, commissioned by
Christian IV and made by Hans
Brokman from Copenhagen is, to be seen
in Roskilde Cathedral. It is made of
sandstone, marble and alabaster, and
adorned with the symbols of the four
evangelists.

TWO CENTRE PIECES
MADE OF AMBER
ROSENBORG, COPENHAGEN

DETAIL

A Roskilde artist named Oluf Krog was responsible for a number of pulpits made for parish churches in the 1580s. They have classical columns, with carved figures of the evangelists. New pews were constructed and placed at right angles to the north and south walls, the southern pews were, for a long time, reserved exclusively for men, the northern ones for women. Many of the pews have elaborate carvings, with panels surmounted by human figures. Some have the coats of arms of prominent citizens. Arguably the most splendid of all the pews was that created for Christian IV in Roskilde Cathedral.

Painting for churches did not of course come to an end with the Reformation. In Ribe Cathedral the old Catholic altar was taken down in a solemn ceremony on Christmas Eve, 1597. It was replaced by a new Renaissance creation incorporating the national coat of arms, a number of relief sculptures and paintings of the Passion by a local artist named Laurenz Andersen Riber.

Christian IV was lavish in commissioning portraits of himself and paintings to decorate the walls and ceilings of his palaces. The artists he chose were predominantly Dutch. He evidently enjoyed seeing himself in the role of conquering warrior, as a portrait by Pieter Isaacsz of Amsterdam, commissioned for Frederiksborg, makes clear. Included in the scene painted is a

CAT'S DOOR
RIBE CATHEDRAL

relief, in which the King appears as a
Roman emperor in a chariot.

Heroic themes and Danish triumphs
depicted in paintings were not restricted
to the glorification of Christian himself.

CRUCIFIX BY GEORG PETEL
MUSEUM OF NATIONAL
HISTORY, FREDERIKSBORG

For Kronborg another Dutch artist, Geraerd van Honthorst, portrayed the King of Sweden surrendering to Queen Margrethe of Denmark.

Stylistically in many of the paintings, for example one showing Aeneas and his followers being attacked by harpies, which was commissioned for Frederiksborg, there is a strong tendency towards mannerism, with striking gestures and contortions of naked bodies.

**TANKARD OF GOLD EMBOSSED
WITH PASTORAL SCENES
ROSENBORG, COPENHAGEN**

For the sculptures he required for his
castles – a portrait bust of himself, a
marble gallery, a fountain – Christian also
turned to Dutch and Flemish artists.
Danish painters and sculptors did, of
course, continue to practise. A number
were organised in guilds. Records show
that Laurenz Andersen Riber was only
one of half-a-dozen professional painters
in his home town of Ribe. Nevertheless,
as a consequence of Christian IV's taste
and his wealth, the monumental works in
architecture, painting and sculpture in
Renaissance or manncrist style to be seen
in Denmark today nearly all have an
evident imprint from the Low Countries.

DETAIL OF GOLD EMBOSSED
TANKARD
ROSENBORG, COPENHAGEN

In thc applied arts in the same period
there was a wealth of beautiful work, as
the contents of Rosenborg abundantly
make clear. In Denmark, as in other
countries in the seventeenth century,
new opportunities for craftsmen were
created by the large influx of silver
which followed the discovery of mines
on the American continent. By the end
of the century even a peasant's home
might well contain a silver cup, although
it was thought reasonable to expect
guests to bring their own spoon and
knife with them. The rich would keep a
number of silver and, perhaps, gold
vessels to be used on special occasions.

Some of the Renaissance silver drinking
vessels made for the rich are startling in
their splendour. One, which can be seen
today in the National Museum in

**DETAIL OF AGATE STANDING
CUP AND COVER
ROSENBORG, COPENHAGEN**

Copenhagen, was presented by Hans Skovgaard, a Privy Councillor, to Christian IV as a christening gift for one of the King's children. It rests on three lions and three pomegranates and is decorated with the coat of arms of Skovgaard and of his wife's family. Another beautiful object is a silver tankard made by an Odense craftsman, which shows animal and floral motifs interspersed with lettering. One inscription in Greek contains the statement that he who drinks much sins often.

A peculiarly Scandinavian form of silver drinking vessel was the kovsken, which was used mainly for the convivial consumption of hot spirits. This was a richly decorated form of tankard. The lids were frequently inset with a contemporary coin. Inside small pegs were inserted, one above another. The pegs indicated how far down a man might drink before passing the tankard to whoever sat next to him. Forfeits were paid, no doubt frequently, for drinking below the level of the peg.

In tapestry too there were remarkable developments. Some Danish houses had from early times been decorated with simple wall paintings and tapestries. Little of this work remains. In St Knud's church in Odense there is a carefully preserved piece of silk-woven material dating from the eleventh century, showing eagles with wings outspread and believed to be of Byzantine origin. But the majority of medieval tapestries which have survived tend to be somewhat crude representations of biblical scenes.

In 1577 an event occurred which was to transform the art of tapestry in Denmark.

This was the establishment in Kronborg castle of a workshop under the control of the Flemish painter and weaver, Hans Knieper. Its most ambitious undertaking was the creation of forty-three tapestries, which decorated the great ballroom in the castle.

More than a hundred Danish monarchs are portrayed, all with their crests and a brief biography in German verse. Frederik II is shown with sceptre, orb and crown. On one side of him is a dog, on the other the youthful figure of the future King Christian IV. Kronborg Castle is in the background. The style of the whole work is a Flemish variation of Italian Renaissance, with an abundance of flowers and fruit, animals and huntsmen. Another tapestry from the same workshop on wool and silk, with gold and silver thread, shows large female figures representing various virtues.

For Christian IV tapestries, like paintings, depicted, among other themes, victory over the Swedes. The King also imported tapestries from the Low Countries, but he gave an important impetus to indigenous tapestry work by establishing a new workshop in Copenhagen,

Another industry which began to flourish in Denmark during the Renaissance, and which in time was to produce work of skilled craftsmanship and aesthetic delight, was lace. In 1619

TAPESTRY SHOWING
CHRISTIAN II
DETAIL
NATIONAL MUSEUM
COPENHAGEN

Christian IV recorded in his diary giving
889 rigsdaler to various tradesmen for
lace and linen. The centre of the lace
industry was already Tønder, where it
was to flourish for centuries to come.

In Denmark the term "renaissance", in its
meaning of new birth, was peculiarly
applicable. In Italy it had signified the
rediscovery of a great classical past. For
the Danes it was the introduction of new
styles and new standards from the Low
Countries and Germany and, to a lesser
extent, from France and Italy. They
enriched castle and church, landscape and
manor-house, painting, sculpture and a
variety of applied arts, blending in time
with established indigenous traditions.

For all this posterity owes Christian IV
an enormous debt. How well he served
his subjects in his lifetime is more
questionable. His political judgments
tended to be ill considered, and his
understanding of economics was
negligible. An ill-advised intervention in
the Protestant cause in the Thirty Years
War was followed by military defeat, the
ceding of territory and the threat of a
burghers' revolt.

When Christian died the crown was in
pawn and the silk covering of his coffin
was obtained on credit. This strange
blend of national near-bankruptcy and a
startling upsurge of art was to be
repeated in Denmark nearly two hundred
years after his death.

DETAIL FROM TAPESTRY
NATIONAL MUSEUM
COPENHAGEN

V.

BAROQUE, ROCOCO AND BEYOND

AMBER CENTRE-PIECE
DETAIL

"Inquire me first what Danskers are in Paris,
And how, and who, what means, and where they keep,
What company, at what expense" –
Polonius, Hamlet

In a garden of about 120 hectares sloping down to Esrum Lake in North Zealand there is a splendid baroque palace. The central section, which is white, of exquisite symmetry and surmounted by green copper roofs, is approached by an avenue, which leads to a circus.

Around this circus are two-storey buildings forming three sides of an octagon. There are twenty-eight buildings in all, including an orangery and a chapel.

The principal architect, Johann Cornelius Krieger, was a landscape gardener employed at Rosenborg Palace, and it was in his blend of a baroque mansion with a baroque garden, having geometric shapes, statuary, mazes and box-edging, that he came near to achieving perfection.

The palace was built to commemorate
the signing of peace between Denmark
and Sweden in 1720 and for that reason
was named Fredensborg. The decision to
build was made by King Frederik IV,
who, at the age of twenty-one, had made
a journey to France and Italy, where he
had been much impressed by Roman
palaces, northern Italian villas and the
gardens of Versailles. Krieger was shown
the designs of the domed assembly room
in the ducal palace in Modena and
instructed to achieve a similar effect.

GOTTFRED WOLFFRAM
AMBER BOX WITH IVORY
RELIEFS SHOWING PASTORAL
SCENES
ROSENBORG, COPENHAGEN

Fredensborg is today the summer residence of the Danish royal family. Another royal palace, Amalienborg, was in part the creation of Niels Eigtved, who may well be adjudged the outstanding Danish rococo architect. New styles were introduced as work on the building continued. Of the palace when completed the distinguished English architectural historian, Sir Banister Fletcher, wrote that it had one of "the most important early neo-classical interiors in Europe."

Eigtved had studied in Saxony and Austria as well as in Rome. He designed, very much under French influence, the Prinsens Palace in Copenhagen as a residence for the future King Frederik V. It had three wings, the centre one backing away from a street adjoining a canal, and an interior court. The building now houses much of the National Museum.

Frederik V engaged Eigtved to work on a plan for a new quarter of Copenhagen, to be known as Frederiksstaden, where the Amalienborg Palace was to be built. The plan, which had its origins a century earlier in the mind of Christian IV, was suggested to Frederik V by Count A.G. Moltke, his artistic adviser, who directed the course of much of the artistic life of Denmark in the mid-eighteenth century.

Eigtved proposed an octagon, which would be surrounded by buildings of similar design and identical height, but his plans were modified by the German architect and painter, Marcus Tuscher, who opted instead for the creation of four separate palaces, each of which would be flanked by a small pavilion. To add to the effect of harmony it was decided that the neighbouring streets should have houses of similar design. The palaces had different owners, Count Moltke being one of them.

The Amalienborg complex was completed by two additions. One was an imposing equestrian statue of Frederik V by the French sculptor, J. F. J. Saly, which shows the King looking out across the square towards a point where boats pass in the background. The other was the erection in 1794 of a classical colonnade in wood. This served to link two of the palaces, which by then had become royal residences. It was the work of C. F. Harsdorff, a Danish neo-classical architect of considerable distinction. Another building designed as a royal residence, but no longer serving as

such, is, like Amalienborg, one of the
visual delights of Copenhagen. It is set
impressively on top of a hill, below
which lies Frederiksberg Park. The park
is a blend of woodlands, canals, Chinese
pavilion, Swiss cottage, peacocks and rose
garden. The palace was conceived as an

J. F. J. SALY

EQUESTRIAN STATUE OF

FREDERIK V

COPENHAGEN

Italianate building in the style of the Aldobrandini villa in Frascati, which Frederik IV remembered well. It has a low roof, triangular pediments alternating with arched ones over the first-floor windows, and a benign-seeming, cream-coloured facade. The south wing was converted into an orangery by Eigtved. Among the interior features are a marble bath designed by Harsdorff under a mirrored ceiling.

Danish kings in the eighteenth century tended to follow Christian IV's example in having splendid new buildings created for the most part in and around Copenhagen. As a consequence it is in the capital that some of the finest baroque architecture in Denmark can be seen. There are indeed exceptions, one of which derives directly from a project of Christian IV.

Late in his life Christian had a castle built for his son Valdemar, choosing as his architect Hans van Steenwinckel, the master of Dutch Renaissance. The site was near Bregninge on a small island off Fyn. Valdemar was killed in battle in 1656, the castle was seriously damaged in the war against the Swedes, and what remained was presented to the Danish naval hero, Niels Juel. The rebuilt castle, still known as Valdemars Slot, is a masterpiece of baroque. The house looks out on to a park and an artificial lake. An exquisite pavilion is placed with perfect judgment between the lake and the sea.

DANISH CROWN

ROSENBORG, COPENHAGEN

JENS JUEL
PORTRAIT OF CHRISTIAN VII
IN HIS CORONATION ROBES
FREDERIKSBORG

The ways in which Fredensborg, Amalienborg and Frederiksberg Palace came into being encapsulate much of what occurred in the more spectacular arts in Denmark in the late seventeenth and eighteenth centuries. Towards the end of the long reign of Christian IV the Dutch Renaissance style first blended with, then began to be replaced by, mannerism and baroque. After his death the state of the economy and the military threat from Sweden were such that fortifications were more urgently needed than palaces. Copenhagen did indeed become a fortified city once more, as it had been in the time of Bishop Absalon.

Under the autocratic rulers in the eighteenth century splendour of design returned. Funds for patronage of the arts were not as readily available as when Christian IV had been at the height of his power. It was even decided that the cost of the Saly statue could not be met from royal resources, and the shortfall was made good by a trading concern. This was the Asiatisk Kompagni, which had had a building with a splendid baroque facade constructed, a building which today houses the Danish Foreign Ministry.

With the commissioning of the Saly statue a practice was begun which in time was to be hugely beneficial to the arts and the artists of Denmark, commercial and industrial patronage.

The tastes of the eighteenth century rulers and their artistic advisers were much more multi-national than in the time of Christian IV. Dutch influence was still to be seen in domestic baroque architecture, with symmetry, harmonious proportions, perpendicular divisions of facades and pilasters. But for guidance in the design of buildings, and in the visual arts generally, patrons and artists increasingly looked further south.

Among the more interesting portraits in the Museum of National History in Frederiksborg Castle is one of Frederik III. It shows a man of thoughtful, perhaps introspective expression, dressed almost entirely in black, with a window and a few flowers in the background. The artist's name is not known, but it is difficult to believe he could have been other than Dutch or Flemish.

The portrait is assumed to have been painted in the 1650s. Some thirty years later the first appointment was made of a Court-Painter-in-Chief. The artist chosen was a Frenchman, Jacques d'Agar, a Protestant, who had spent some time in England, where he had become familiar with the portraits of royalty and nobility painted by Peter Lely.

Agar painted Christian V in a number of guises. In one he is a Roman emperor. In another he is in coronation robes. The general effect is to suggest theatrical costumery, albeit on an impressive scale. The contrast with the portrait of a thoughtful Frederik III could hardly be greater.

Danish kings continued to invite portrait painters from other European countries throughout the eighteenth century. Among them was Johann Dahl, who came to Denmark from Hamburg, and in whose portraits of royalty there is a solemnity, which verges at times on grandeur. But gradually indigenous talent came to be recognised.

A significant event was the establishment in Copenhagen in 1738 of the Royal Academy of Arts, of which Moltke was President for sixteen years. In 1748 it was enlarged to include a school of architecture. Five years later the Academy was installed in a royal palace.

One of the Academy's most gifted painter-pupils was a Swede by birth, Carl Gustav Pilo, who came to Denmark as a

DETAIL OF A ROOM IN
ROSENBORG, COPENHAGEN

A ROOM IN ROSENBORG,
COPENHAGEN

young man to escape a marriage which he regretted. There is a lightness of touch, an almost impressionistic sense of spontaneity and a feeling for colour in his portraits, lacking in many of the earlier court paintings.

In the work of one Danish painter, Jens Juel, the break-out from the prevailing rococo style of the late eighteenth century can be clearly seen. A portrait painter patronised by a number of aristocrats, he had an evident feeling for nature and an ability to portray it convincingly. In his picture of a thunderstorm building up behind a farmhouse in Zealand he gave a clear indication of what was to follow in Danish painting in the next century.

Duty and pleasure demanded of royal patrons not only that they should have their portraits painted, but that the best available artists should decorate the walls and ceilings of their palaces.

Christian IV had set an example in Rosenborg by having landscape paintings set into panelling, by trompe l'oeil marble slabs, and by the portrayal of Jupiter and Juno disporting themselves on the ceiling. The tradition was continued in Frederiksberg, where two Danish-born painters left clear imprints.

One of them, Heinrich Krock, who had studied in Italy and at the Académie des Beaux Arts in Paris, covered ceilings with extravagant compositions featuring allegorical and mythological figures. His painting on the ceiling of the Frederiksberg chapel of the Adoration of the Lamb of the Apocalypse gives an impression of perpetual circular motion.

On one of the castle ceilings a painting by Bernard le Coffre, who was born in the same year, 1671, as Krock, creates a similar sensation of circular motion. The subject is a fancy-dress ball with a large cast of dancers and musicians.

In Amalienborg, amid gilt rococo ornamentation, there are allegories of art and science painted on double doors by the richly gifted François Boucher, favourite artist of Madame de Pompadour. But, as in the palace's architecture, so too in its decor the transition from rococo to neo-classical can be seen in startling clarity.

The decoration of the dining-room in the mansion once belonging to Count Moltke was supervised by a French architect, Nicolas-Henri Jardin, who had spent some time in Rome. There he had become acquainted with the work of Piranesi, whose prints of the classical buildings of Rome were so hugely

GOLDEN CHALICE

THE ENGRAVING ON THE

CHALICE IS BASED ON

ILLUSTRATIONS MADE FOR

THE STRASBOURG EDITION OF

LUTHER'S BIBLE

ROSENBORG, COPENHAGEN

influential in the development of neo-classicism throughout Europe. The room is divided into three parts, but linked by columns, on top of which are classical vases crowned with leaves. Opulence of candelabra and fountain are offset by naturalistic portrayal of flora. The prevailing impression is of dignity and spaciousness.

The practice of installing pulpits, which the Reformation fostered, afforded a number of Danish baroque and rococo artists and craftsmen opportunities to enrich their churches. One example of their work is the mid-seventeenth century baroque pulpit in St Hans Church in Odense made by a local wood carver. The scenes portrayed include the Annunciation, the Baptism, the Circumcision and the twelve-year-old Jesus in the temple. A hundred years later in another Odense church, St Knuds, a rococo pulpit was created, also by a local wood carver. Here the panels show a variety of Christian symbols and other objects, among them a serpent and an apple, a cross, a chalice and a trumpet.

For a quick appreciation of how fashions in carvings in churches developed in Denmark from the advent of the baroque a visitor might be well advised to study the royal tombs in Roskilde Cathedral. Those of Frederik III, who died in 1670, and his Queen Sophie Amalie are made of polished copper, with brass mouldings and ornaments. The lids are decorated with a crucifix and angels. There are busts of both King and Queen, his adorned with weapons and captured prisoners, hers with figures representing hope and wisdom. Lengthy inscriptions in Latin sing the praises of both monarchs.

The motifs on the tombs of Christian V, who died in 1699, and his Queen are taken from the Rosenborg tapestries. Two naval battles are depicted, there are figures representing justice and peace, and more panegyrics in Latin. As are those of Frederik III and his Queen the tombs are the work of artists from the Low Countries.

The tomb of Christian VI, by contrast, who died in 1746, was designed some twenty years later by the Danish neo-classical sculptor, Johannes Wiedeweldt. It is made of white Italian marble and is placed on the backs of four sphinxes. The King is portrayed as a Roman emperor and is confronted by a figure of Pallas Athene.

JENS JUEL

LANDSCAPE IN LATE

AFTERNOON LIGHT

NY CARLSBERG GLYPTOTEK

Saly's equestrian statue in the
Amalienborg Square, reminiscent in both
conception and design of that of Marcus
Aurelius in the Capitol in Rome, had an
evident influence on the development of
Danish neo-classical sculpture. In 1754
Saly was appointed Director of the Royal
Academy.

Pupils at the Academy competed for
various prizes and medals, the most
valued award being the financing of a
period of study in Italy or France. In the
year in which Saly became Director
Johannes Wiedeweldt began a four-year
period of study in Rome. He returned a
dedicated neo-classicist, a number of
whose statues now adorn the gardens at

BERTEL THORVALDSEN
CUPID AND PSYCHE
THORVALDSENS MUSEUM
COPENHAGEN

Fredensborg. One is an impressively
brooding figure representing winter.
Another, based on a globe, is a
monument to the great Danish
astronomer, Tycho Brahe.

Wiedeweldt was a theoretician as well as
a practising artist, and in a book
significantly entitled "Thoughts on Taste

in the Arts in General" he encouraged others to follow where Saly had led. Painters too took the road to Rome, prominent among them being Nicolai Abildgaard, whose neo-classical works, often inspired by literary themes, can be seen in some numbers in the National Museum for Fine Arts in Copenhagen. Study in Rome became indeed as formative an influence for Danish artists as study in Paris would be in a later age.

BERTEL THORVALDSEN,
FIGURES

A more distinguished sculptor than Wiedefeldt, Bertel Thorvaldsen, arrived in Rome on 8th March, 1797, later stating that up to that moment he had not been born.

BERTEL THORVALDSEN,
FIGURES

The artistic world of Rome was then somewhat dominated by Antonio Canova, whose standing as a sculptor was such that Pope Clement XIII conferred on him the titles of Marquis of Ischia and Prefect of the Fine Arts. Canova was generous in his praise of Thorvaldsen, describing one of his early and ambitious creations, Jason with the Golden Fleece, as having been fashioned in "a new and grandiose style." Of Thorvaldsen's Adonis he declared that it was "noble, beautiful and full of sentiment." He even described the artist as "a divine being."

It was Thorvaldsen's Jason which enabled him to continue working in Rome. His grant had come to an end, and a carriage was waiting to take him away when a rich English collector, Thomas Hope, called at his studio, ordered a new version of Jason in marble, and paid in advance. For the next forty years Thorvaldsen continued working in Rome, where he was generally recognised as the central figure among a number of Danish artists. His international reputation grew steadily, the Crown Prince of Bavaria stating that there were many kings, but only one Thorvaldsen.

The bulk of his work consisted of figures from classical antiquity and portrait-busts. One of his busts was of Lord Byron, who complained that it did not make him look sufficiently unhappy. Another, of Schiller, was cast in bronze and erected in the Schillerplatz in Stuttgart.

The name of Canova readily conjures up a picture of calm and self-assurance, of white marble, smooth and curvaceous. Thorvaldsen's sculpture has a similar immediate effect. Both were esteemed in their lifetime for having replaced the excesses of rococo by recreating the ancient classical style derived from masters such as Praxitiles. Posterity has tended to take a less generous view, but that the work of both artists has a quality of grandeur can hardly be denied.

There were differences in their techniques. Canova would polish the marble and rub in wax to give an impression of translucence. Thorvaldsen preferred a somewhat rougher finish with only a little polishing to achieve a slight gleam. Canova's figures seem often to have been caught in mid-movement. Thorvaldsen's are more restful and relaxed.

To achieve his effects Thorvaldsen began with sketches which seem to have been hurriedly executed. These were followed by small models in clay, perhaps a metre high. Happily a large number of both sketches and models have been preserved and can be seen today in the museum in Copenhagen devoted to Thorvaldsen's work. There is a vigour, even a restlessness, in many of the sketches which are in interesting contrast with the apparent calm of the final products.

The creation of a museum to house the work of a single artist was a novelty in Denmark and an indication of the esteem in which Thorvaldsen was held in his lifetime. When he was finally persuaded to

leave Rome a naval vessel was sent by the
Danish Government to bring him home.

The design of the museum was entrusted
to a young architect, Gottlieb
Bindesbøll, whom Thorvaldsen regarded
highly. Frederik VI agreed to present a
site near Christianborg Palace, where a
coach-house had stood, and a neo-
classical building of considerable
distinction arose. Ionic pillars, a
triumphal arch, a Greek-style temple
entrance, a painted frieze depicting
chariot-racing, and ceiling decorations
illustrating Thorvaldsen's work
complement the main exhibits. The
whole represents the undisputed
triumph of neo-classicism in Danish art.

Thorvaldsen's work is to be seen
elsewhere in Denmark: in a park in
Aalborg, a font in Horne, an altarpiece
in Hørsholm, even a statue of Christian
IV in Roskilde Cathedral. But outside
the Thorvaldsen Museum the most
striking examples are in the Copenhagen
Cathedral, which was recreated in neo-
classical style after being severely
damaged by the British bombardment in
1807.

One of these is the figure of Christ
forming the altarpiece. Another is the
font in which a kneeling angel is seen
holding a shell. Thorvaldsen's Christ is far
removed from crucifixion or suffering,
He might be thought a distinguished
preacher or even an elder statesman.

DONOR PORTRAITS, SHOWING
THE DONORS THEMSELVES
AND THEIR FAMILIES, WERE
GIFTS MADE TO CHURCHES BY
WEALTHY WORSHIPPERS.
DETAILS
AARHUS CATHEDRAL

During the baroque age, and the period of transition through rococo towards neo-classicism which followed, work of distinction, in which the eye can delight today, was created in Denmark in a number of the applied arts. That this was so becomes immediately evident to the visitor to the Hall of the Knights in Rosenborg.

An exhibit which immediately catches the eye in this room is the throne used for the coronation of all Danish kings between 1671 and 1840. It is made of narwhal ivory, with allegorical figures of gilt bronze. Three silver lions guard the throne.

Elsewhere there is a figure of Mars made of chalcedony with gold armour. A leather saddle is covered with black velvet and has gold embroidery with pearls, diamonds and sapphires. A gold chalice is partly covered with open-work gold and enamel ornaments. A prayer-book is bound in gold and enamel with, as motifs in relief, flowers and coats-of-arms. Glass figures represent commedia dell'arte characters. There is a tureen in soft-paste porcelain with lapis lazuli ground and golden ornamentation. There is also a guitar made of wood, tortoise-shell and ivory veneer.

Gold boxes became standard gifts at court, an outstanding example which has survived being a rococo enamelled one, also to be seen in Rosenborg. Silversmiths produced some exquisite vessels for tea, chocolate and coffee with fluted decorations. Other silver cups and bowls were lined with blue glass.

Weaving was a skill practised by both royalty and peasants. Armchairs embroidered with Chinese motifs by Queen Charlotte and a number of other court ladies at the end of the seventeenth century are still to be seen. Dutch settlers in Amager had a distinctive style, decorating linen panels with cross-stitching in silk, cotton or wool.

In another form of applied art, ceramics, Denmark began in the eighteenth century to produce work which before long would acquire international fame. The first Danish faience factory was established in Store Kongensgade in Copenhagen, at the expense of King Frederik IV, in 1722. The aim was to produce a Danish equivalent of the blue-painted Delft wares.

ROYAL THRONE WITH
ANNOINTING MANTLE
ROSENBORG, COPENHAGEN

The enterprise began badly, the first director of the factory promptly removing himself, his principal painter and his stock of cobalt blue to Sweden. But before long, under the artistic management of Johan Ernst Pfau, work of quality was being produced. Among the products were a blue-painted punch bowl shaped like a bishop's mitre and a tray with an engagingly rococo chinoiserie design. Another was a hexagonal plate decorated with a profusion of leaves and signed with the monogram "JP."

A more ambitious venture followed a decision to engage in the ancient Chinese craft of porcelain-making, an

FLORA DANICA
ROYAL COPENHAGEN

understanding of which did not reach Europe until the end of the seventeenth century.

In 1775 a factory established under the patronage of the Dowager Queen Juliane Marie began making real, or hard-paste, porcelain. At the inaugural general meeting held that year it was decided that the factory's distinctive mark would be three wavy blue lines. These symbolised the waterways surrounding and dividing Denmark, the Sound and the Great and Little Belts.

FLORA DANICA
ROYAL COPENHAGEN

From the outset it was decided to concentrate on the manufacture of the kind of porcelain that was painted before firing took place. This was at 1400 degrees Celsius, and when the Copenhagen factory came into being the only colour known to be able to endure such a temperature was cobalt blue. It was a substance used by potters in Mesopotamia to produce blue glaze as early as the ninth century. Cobalt was also used by the Chinese in the making of blue Ming porcelain.

Other colours could have been used by adding the decorations after the firing, but one of the most expensive items in production costs at that time was the large quantity of wood needed to heat the kilns. As the firing would have to be done repeatedly after the colours had been painted, cost-analysis showed the compelling advantages of cobalt blue.

FLUTE PLAYER
ROYAL COPENHAGEN

The principal patterns then established were to be sustained over two centuries in Royal Copenhagen porcelain. One was known as blue-fluted, the other as blue flower. The blue-fluted pattern was derived from the stylised chrysanthemum to be seen on some Chinese porcelain. There are three different varieties of it: plain with an unadorned border, half-lace with a painted border, and full lace with a cut-out lace border. The blue flower pattern, which dates from 1779, has a number of variations in both the shape and positioning of the pattern. These are known as curved, braided and angular.

Although a policy of conservatism served it well, the Copenhagen factory also engaged in one of the most ambitious undertakings in the history of porcelain manufacture. This was the Flora Danica service.

Its origins are to be found in an encyclopedic work, whose first volume appeared in 1761. This illustrated and described all the wild flowers of the kingdom. As the kingdom at that time included Norway, Denmark and a considerable area later incorporated in Germany, the climatic range was considerable and the variety of wild flowers correspondingly extensive.

A porcelain service showing these flowers was commissioned in 1790 by the future King Frederik VI, then Crown

Prince. No fewer than 1,802 hand-
moulded and hand-painted pieces were
produced as a result, an exercise taking
twelve years to complete. Pimpernel,
monkshood, viola, arctic bramble,
saxifrage, speedwell, cinquefoil and a vast
range of other wild flowers adorned a
unique porcelain service. A characteristic
feature of the different pieces in the set
was a garland of pearls on the segregated
edges.

There were political considerations, as
well as a desire for artistic extravagance,
giving rise to the Flora Danica service. It
was almost certainly intended as a gift to
the Empress Catherine of Russia,
probably as a peace-offering rather than a
simple gesture of goodwill.

The Empress died before she could
receive it, and the Flora Danica service
remained with the Royal Danish
household. More than 1,500 pieces of
the original set have been preserved.
Some are kept for use on state occasions.
The rest, the great majority, is on display
in Rosenborg.

DETAIL OF GOLDEN CHALICE

ROSENBORG, COPENHAGEN

VI.

THE GOLDEN AGE AND AFTER

"Look here, upon this picture, and on this."
– Hamlet

C.W. ECKERSBERG
DETAIL OF WOMAN STANDING
IN FRONT OF MIRROR
HIRSCHSPRUNG COLLECTION
COPENHAGEN

In the seventeenth and eighteenth centuries Denmark learnt much, absorbed much and adapted much from the main cultural stream of western and southern Europe. (So indeed did other northern countries, England among them.) In the nineteenth century a new and distinctively Danish style of art was created. One medium through which it was memorably expressed was painting.

This characteristically Danish art came into being, not in a period of national triumph, but in one of humiliation and of the resentment which such humiliation engenders. In 1795 a devastating fire broke out in Copenhagen, destroying upwards of a thousand buildings. Twelve years later damage on a comparable scale was caused by a bombardment ordered by Sir Arthur Wellesley, later Duke of Wellington, who

C.W. ECKERSBERG

DOUBLE PORTRAIT OF COUNT

PREBEN BILLE-BRAHE AND

HIS SECOND WIFE, JOHANNE

CAROLINE

NY CARLSBERG GLYPTOTEK,

COPENHAGEN

may be thought to have compounded the offence by naming his favourite horse Copenhagen. In 1813 the state of Denmark was declared bankrupt. The next year Denmark was obliged to cede Norway to Sweden under the terms of the Treaty of Vienna.

There were student meetings and demonstrations, but there was a minimum of violence and no uprising of the people. Instead among artists of various kinds, poets and dramatists, musicians and painters, there was a widespread sense of a need to create work through which national regeneration could be expressed.

How this was achieved by painters was influenced to a remarkable extent by the nature of the Danish countryside. In a number of European countries in the nineteenth century mountains became symbols of much of the romantic, nationalist movement in art. Denmark was not one of them, for Denmark has no mountains.

For a true appreciation of much Danish visual art it is indeed necessary to understand that to the Danes the absence of mountains is not a deprivation, but a source of strength. In 1842 the gifted young painter Thomas Lundbye was to give expression to this feeling when he wrote: "I have made it my aim to paint our beloved Denmark in all its simplicity and modesty – what beauty is to be seen in the fine lines of our hills, so gently undulating."

The term which posterity has, by common consent, applied to the work of the generation of painters of whom Lundbye was one is the Golden Age of Danish painting. In the formulation of theories and their translation into art the Golden Age painters had a guide of exceptional authority. This was Christoffer Wilhelm Eckersberg, who, like Thorvaldsen and Weideweldt and Abildgaard, had learnt much from a prolonged stay in Rome, but who was led by what he had learnt into new directions.

Eckersberg painted a number of urban scenes in Rome. They are realistic, even in the smallest details, yet he was selective in his realism. He was to insist, when he returned to Denmark, that artists must paint what they saw, but it was what they chose to see that dictated the nature of their work. In his painting of the marble steps leading up to Santa Maria in Aracoeli, for example, he omitted all the high renaissance and baroque buildings, recreating instead, with extreme accuracy, a largely medieval scene.

When Eckersberg returned to Denmark he very soon occupied a position of authority. In 1816 he was appointed Professor at the Royal Academy of Fine Arts, and for more than thirty years he guided those whom he

THOMAS LUNDBYE
LANDSCAPE AT ARRESØ
NY CARLSBERG GLYPTOTEK,
COPENHAGEN

initiated into the Golden Age. He took
young artists into the countryside around
Copenhagen to study and paint, and he
encouraged the use of nude models, both
novel practices at the time. He preferred
painting in full daylight and insisted on
meticulous accuracy in detail.

As an artist himself Eckersberg was both
prolific and versatile. His painting of a
woman in front of a mirror, perhaps the
best known of all his works, suggests a
Venus of the bourgeoisie, the partial front
view in the mirror being rather more
provocative than the fuller back view
before it. In his picture of a Russian ship
at anchor off Helsingør it is not difficult
to guess how he did in fact paint it,
beginning with the sky, which dominates
all, then the outline of the sailing ship,
then the vast intricacy of detail.

Eckersberg was fortunate in that among those Danes who prospered in the second quarter of the nineteenth century there was a growing fashion for having their portraits painted. Just as it was thought desirable to set aside rooms in which little happened and children were not allowed, so it was thought fit to adorn such rooms with family portraits. Eckersberg, as a result, painted husband, wife and all eight children of a merchant family in Copenhagen named Nathanson.

The very accuracy Eckersberg insisted on happily precluded him from being too flattering. A portrait painted in 1830, for example, shows a girl, perhaps in her late teens, with a purple dress embroidered with lace, a smooth hair-style and holding a pink rose. A close appraisal suggests she will grow in time into a formidable female not to be provoked lightly.

Eckersberg may not have been touched by genius, but it is at least arguable that two of the Golden Age painters, Christen Købke and Thomas Lundbye, were. Both died young, Købke at the age of thirty-eight. Lundbye, when he was only thirty, was killed shortly after volunteering to fight in the war against Prussia in 1848.

In his teachings Eckersberg led Danish artists away from the mythical, the grandiose, the allegorical, directing their attention instead to what was immediately in front of them. Købke's paintings are an abiding justification of Eckersberg's doctrines.

Købke led a thoroughly unadventurous life. He was the son of a master baker and, even after marrying, he lived in his father's home. To find subjects to paint he only occasionally ventured beyond Copenhagen and its immediate surroundings, and it was with some reluctance that he made a comparatively brief journey to Dresden and Rome. The backyard of his father's bakery and the steps leading up to his own studio provided him with inspiration enough.

Perhaps the most famous of Købke's paintings is of a street in a suburb of Copenhagen. Cows contentedly cross the road. Women in black, except for their linen head-dresses, gossip. The street is lined with poplars, and prominent in the centre of it is a pump.

For one of his portraits Købke chose as his subject a fellow-artist and friend, Frederik Sødring. The outcome is a blend of portrait and still life which has led a distinguished critic to suggest that the most obvious comparison must be with the work of Vermeer. Sødring's brocaded waistcoat and linen shirt are in striking contrast with the greys of the sketches on the wall behind him. Leaves climb up from a pot on a console table, and standing out against the generally muted colours is a small scarlet box. The viewer must surely be aware of the unseen presence of Købke, with whom Sødring is carrying on a conversation.

Lundbye was not so directly influenced by Eckersberg as Købke was. He

DETAIL

CHRISTEN KØBKE
NORTH GATE OF THE CITADEL
NY CARLSBERG GLYPTOTEK,
COPENHAGEN

absorbed the doctrine of meticulous observation, but there was a romantic element in his representation, which derived from his deeply felt patriotism. In one painting he replaced the stone wall of reality with a burial mound intended to evoke Denmark's past.

It is the countryside of Zealand, the people who work in it and the light which suffuses it that Lundbye so effectively recreates. In one painting of cows being watered at a village pond there are low-roofed farmhouses and undulating fields, their contours emphasised by cloud effects. In a painting whose subject is shifting sand dunes a cow, some sheep and a farm-worker are in the foreground.

The light which Lundbye conveys is a very Danish one. Whereas in other countries lakes are commonly

P.S.KRØYER
BOYS BATHING AT SKAGEN
NATIONAL MUSEUM FOR
FINE ARTS, COPENHAGEN

surrounded by mountains, in Denmark
what the eye sees – most vividly at sunset
– may be a thin pencil of land dividing
water and sky. Such a light is made to
prevail in a number of Lundbye's
paintings by the device of giving over the
upper half or two thirds of the canvas to
the sky. In a painting of the Ile inlet land
and sea, a fishing-boat and two figures in
the water are confined to a thin strip at
the bottom. The rest is light grey and
faintly pink sky with wispy clouds.

DETAIL

In the Golden Age of Danish painting the
centre of activity was Copenhagen, and
the landscapes portrayed were
predominantly in Zealand. Artists of
course continued to travel.

Martinus Rørbye made a journey to
Greece in the mid-1830s and painted
what he saw painstakingly and vividly. Yet
in his grouping of Greeks fetching water
from a well under a ruined tower there is
something curiously reminiscent of his
better known painting of well dressed
figures outside Copenhagen prison.

DETAIL

Rørbye, a prolific artist, was to some
extent responsible for a change in source
of inspiration and, consequently, in style
which took place in the best Danish
painting after the middle of the century.

In 1833 he visited Skagen in the extreme
north of Jutland. Skagen is an ancient
market town, where fishermen have plied
their trade over the centuries. It has the

largest shifting sand dune in Denmark and yellow houses with red tiled roofs. Every year, it is estimated, 100,000 vessels pass by it. Most important, for painters, it has conditions of light hardly to be seen elsewhere and reflected, at times brilliantly, where the North Sea and the Baltic meet.

Rørbye returned to Skagen fourteen years after his first visit, and by the 1870s an artists' colony had been established there, mostly of Danes, but with some Norwegians. They painted the sea and the fishermen and the people whose livelihood depended on the fishing. One picture shows a young girl reading the Bible to an old lady in an alcove. Another shows the scene in a grocer's shop on a day when no fishing could take place.

The man who may well be adjudged outstanding among the Skagen painters was P. S. Krøyer, who had studied in Paris, learnt the skills of plein-air painting, and come to admire the French impressionists. Much of this is evident in his work, not least his portrayal of the blue of twilight, in which he depicted fishermen hauling on their nets and children and old women making their way across the seashore.

There is a quality in Krøyer's paintings which must arrest the visitor to any of the galleries in Denmark where his work is shown. One picture, to be seen in Odense, for example is a portrait of a white-haired woman sitting in front of a stove spinning. She has a green skirt and a scarf with red borders. The light seems to fall, almost alternately, on her skirt, her hair and one half of her face. It is a lined face, which has never known cosmetics.

Among Krøyer's best known paintings is one of a group of Scandinavian artists lunching in a Skagen hotel. Today a museum close to the hotel houses many of the finest works of Skagen paintings. It was in this hotel that Anna Ancher, who was to become a pioneer of modern Danish art and a brilliant colourist, was born. In her early work she was considerably under Krøyer's influence.

Anna Ancher had a peculiar mastery of light, as shown in her painting of a maid in a kitchen looking towards a window, through which light is streaming in. Of her landscapes and seascapes one of the most impressive

shows a missionary preaching, with sand-
dunes in the background. Some thirty
people are listening with varying degrees
of concentration and conviction.

In the work of both Krøyer and Ancher
the transition from the prevailing style of
the Golden Age towards impressionism
begins to be evident. It is even more
apparent in that of Vilhelm Hammershøi,
a late nineteenth, early twentieth century
artist, who enjoyed considerable
international esteem. Diaghilev
commissioned work from him, and there
were major exhibitions of his paintings in
Berlin and Hamburg. It was even
suggested that Renoir's famous *Baigneuse*
might have been influenced by him.

Hammershøi led a life which was little
more adventurous than that of Købke.
His paintings are mainly of interiors, the

CHRISTEN KØBKE
AUTUMN MORNING
NY CARLSBERG GLYPTOTEK,
COPENHAGEN

dominant shades being black and white and grey. A white chair is placed facing a grey wall. The figure seated on the chair is dressed in black and seen from behind. It was the kind of work which caused him and other artists who would acquire fame in the twentieth century, such as J.F. Willumsen, to have their work shown in what was revealingly called Den Frie. This was a Danish avant-garde exhibition, which was staged in 1891 and was to be highly influential.

The history of Danish painting is exceptional in that its Golden Age occurred around the middle of the nineteenth century. In a number of European countries this was a period which more readily gave rise to the would-be art associated with the fictional figure of Gottlieb Biedermeier: portraits in which details of costume are

all-important, illustrations of myths and
fairy-tales.

There was of course Biedermeier work
in Denmark. A style of genre painting,
for instance, enjoyed considerable
popularity, one of its acknowledged
leaders, Christen Dalsgaard, choosing as
the subject of one of his better known
paintings two Mormons visiting a Danish
carpenter's house. It may be possible to
create great art with such a theme, but it
is unlikely.

Destruction by fire and bombardment in
the late eighteenth and early nineteenth
centuries served to give the city of
Copenhagen much of the appearance it

MARBLE CHURCH, INTERIOR
COPENHAGEN

has today. When Wellington's army had completed its work neo-classicism was at the height of its popularity, and its best practitioners seized the opportunities they were given.

Another direct consequence of destruction was a broadening of squares and streets. Experience of fires had shown how difficult it was for the fire brigade to operate in narrow streets, and in the replanning which took place in the early nineteenth century an enlightened city surveyor and architect, J. W. Ravert, insisted on the creation of new squares. As part of his plan the Town Hall was relocated so that it served to divide two squares from each other.

The design of the new Town Hall, which was combined with the Law Courts, was entrusted to C. F. Hansen, who had succeeded Harsdorff as the most eminent of Danish neo-classical architects. The outcome was a building of perfect harmony of facade, to which the entrance, with broad steps and pillared loggia, gives an imposing dignity. Hansen's many other assignments in Copenhagen included the rebuilding of Copenhagen Cathedral and of Christiansborg Palace. In neither did he seek to recreate or copy an original structure.

The cathedral (Vor Frue Kirke) dates back to the late twelfth century and was a casualty of fire and bombardment. Hansen's building is entered past Doric columns. The plan is similar to that of a Roman temple and so affords Thorvaldsen's impressive statues an appropriate setting. Harmony and dignity prevail throughout the building.

Christiansborg Palace was a baroque structure built on the orders of Christian VI on the site of Bishop Absalon's ancient fortress. The building which stands there today houses the Danish Parliament. After the baroque palace had gone up in flames Hansen was commissioned to design a new one, which he did in his familiar neo-classical style. Here, too, open space added dignity to the whole.

Another fire in 1884 destroyed Hansen's collection almost entirely, and much rebuilding had to be done. An interesting feature of the present structure, which is faced with granite slabs, is that the plinth is made up of 7,000 boulders presented by 720 Danish boroughs.

CONSERVATORY
NY CARSLBERG GLYPTOTEK,
COPENHAGEN

Hansen's work is widely apparent in
Copenhagen, but Harsdorff, who was
appointed a professor at the Royal
Academy as early as 1766, was no less
influential in giving Copenhagen its neo-
classical character. King Christian VI paid
him a considerable compliment by
presenting him with a property next to
Charlottenborg. Here Harsdorff built a
mansion which, he hoped, would serve as
a guide to aspiring architects. Calm and
imposing, it combines symmetry with
three different types of facade and two
different roof surfaces.

DETAIL

The best known of Hansen's creations are to be found in Copenhagen, but he also embellished other Danish towns. Among them is Åbenrå, where he supervised the reconstruction, to his own design, of Brundlund Castle, which had been built in the reign of Margrethe I. He also created a neo-classical town hall in the main square. The town hall in Præstø and the museum in Pederstrup are also his work, so too is the brilliantly light chapel in Roskilde Cathedral, which contains the tomb of Frederick V fashioned by Wiedeweldt.

In Denmark, as elsewhere in Europe, adherence to the precepts of the classical past could not survive the onslaught of new and revived styles influenced by national and romantic feelings. In architecture, as in other arts, historicism and national romanticism were to leave abiding evidence of their vogue.

Copenhagen University, historicist in style, has brick facades mostly derived from medieval Italy. The medieval-style Eliaskirken in Vesterbro has twin turrets. The church was the creation of Martin Nyrop, a leading architect of the national romantic school, who deplored the extensive use of stucco and advocated what he considered the genuine materials of wood, brick and slate.

More startling than either of these is the building which houses the greatest collection of international art to be found in Denmark, the Ny Carlsberg Glyptotek. The building, whose principal architect was Vilhelm Dahlerup, was opened in 1897. Patterned red brickwork provides a background for granite columns, and in the interior much of the ground floor consists of a luxuriant winter garden under a glass domed roof. Inspiration was deemed to have come from a Venetian palace.

Additions to the Glyptotek were made shortly after its opening to the designs of an architect, whose work may well today be considered outstanding among his Danish contemporaries. This was Hack Kampmann, who created something of a masterpiece in the theatre in Aarhus. The facade is neo-classical, there are neo-romanesque motifs, and highly theatrical figures appear on the frieze. The interior has an abundance of painting and an abundance of light. It is a theatre in which actors and actresses are delighted to perform.

OPERA GLASSES OWNED BY
COUNTESS DANNER, THIRD
WIFE OF FREDERIK VII
ROSENBORG, COPENHAGEN

In Danish churches, once neo-classicism ceased to be in vogue, much of the best nineteenth work took the form of reconstruction and adaptation of originals. Outstanding in size and in splendour of concept is, surely, the rebuilt granite Romanesque cathedral in Viborg. The man who most abundantly left his imprint on it was Peter Skovgaard, son of a Golden Age painter of some distinction. The most immediate impressions a visitor to the cathedral is likely to have is of a profusion of paint and of precision in its use. In the nave and in one of the two aisles frescoes tell the story of the Old Testament. The life of Christ is portrayed in the transept. the Resurrection and the Ascension in the choir. On the ceiling above the nave the multiplicity of haloes almost suggests artificial light.

The whole has been described as a unique Protestant pictorial Bible, but, happily, it lacks the sternness of the more extreme forms of Protestantism. The disciples at the Last Supper might be thought earnest students listening to a very young professor. Even Judas, disappearing surreptitiously, seems to be behaving no worse than a soldier going absent without leave.

In some respects no less startling than Skovgaard's paintings in Viborg is the Marble Church in Copenhagen. The original plans for a church were drawn up by Eigtved, the rococo architect involved with the Amalienborg project. After a number of false starts the building was completed in 1874 to the design of Ferdinand Meldahl, who drew his inspiration from St Peter's in Rome and St Paul's in London. It has a massive, copper-coloured dome, one of the largest in Europe, which on the inside is encircled by arcading. There is a rich variety of figures from the Bible and from Danish church history.

The variety of styles succeeding each other with some rapidity in Denmark in the second half of the nineteenth century was not, on the whole, conducive to the production of great work in the applied arts. There were talented artists, who were versatile enough to master a number of skills. One such was Thorvald Bindesbøll, architect of the Thorvaldsen Museum, who designed ceramics, silver, furniture, books and textiles. Round surfaces and bold patterns, particularly in black and white, are characteristic of his work.

CANDELABRA BY ARNOLD KROG, KROG'S ORIGINAL DRAWING
ROYAL COPENHAGEN

Arguably, it was in porcelain that some of the best late nineteenth century work was produced. Important changes in production methods and the development of new styles followed the appointment of Arnold Krog as artistic director of the Royal Copenhagen factory in 1885.

Krog was an architect by profession, who had worked on the restoration of Frederiksborg Castle. He had learnt much from both European and oriental art.

At an experimental workshop he developed a new painting technique, which was particularly effective in making use of Japanese designs. The porcelain, before being fired, was covered in blue. This was partially removed, and the whiteness that was disclosed became an essential part of the decoration.

Krog proved to be a technical innovator of resource and imagination, who brought new life to established patterns and extended their range appreciably. Another of his innovations was the use of a feldspar glaze and firing at extremely high temperatures, which allowed new gradations of colour to be developed.

The vases, urns and figurines produced under Krog's guidance helped to bring Copenhagen porcelain a new international renown. This was shown by the prizes conferred at the World Exhibition in Paris in 1900.

ARNOLD KROG
BLUE AND WHITE VASE
ROYAL COPENHAGEN

Under Krog's guidance Royal Copenhagen maintained its blend of conservatism and innovation. A visitor to the factory's own show-cases today will see a wealth of blue-fluted and blue-flower patterns as well as Flora Danica pieces of the kind once reserved for royalty. Also on display will be landscapes and seascapes. One plate, for example, shows a sailing-boat with, as background, the castle of Hamlet's Elsinore.

In the nineteenth century the practice and enjoyment of the visual arts in Denmark was greatly extended, both geographically and across the social hierarchy. There were comparable changes in the forms of patronage.

There have been three great patrons of the arts in Denmark, the Catholic Church until the Reformation, the Crown for the next two and a half centuries, and subsequently industry. In patronage by industry Denmark has been and is exceptionally fortunate.

An early example of industrial patronage was the financing of the J. F. J. Saly equestrian statue in Amalienborg Square by the Kompagni Asiatisk. The Marble Church in Copenhagen was completed at the expense of a financier, Carl Frederik Tietgen. Krøyer was among a number of artists enabled to travel through the enlightened support of a tobacco manufacturer, Heinrich Hirschsprung. Today the most representative selection of Golden Age paintings is to be found in the museum in Copenhagen which Hirschsprung founded in 1911 and which is known as the Hirschsprung Collection.

On a much more magnificent scale has been the patronage of Carlsberg. In 1888 Carl Jacobsen, son of the founder of the brewing enterprise, and his wife donated their impressive art collection to the Danish nation. Eight years later the New Carlsberg Foundation was created. Its aims. among others, were described as being "the founding of the New Carlsberg Glyptotek and other museums, providing works of art and constructing monumental buildings."

It was a pronouncement which was followed by the making, to date, of nearly 20,000 grants, the excavation of the mausoleum in Halicarnassus and the institution of a much coveted international prize for architecture. In Copenhagen the best known of the gifts is the Little Mermaid sculpture created by Edvard Eriksen in 1913, though countless visitors to the city must have stood and admired the vibrant, curvaceous Neptune fountain, a close copy of the one originally donated by Christian IV. Frederiksborg Castle is an example of a monumental building under the Carlsberg Foundation's perpetual care.

VII.

INTO A NEW CENTURY

"Where is the beauteous majesty of Denmark?" – Ophelia, Hamlet

HENRY HEERUP
DETAIL FROM NAT OG DAG
MUSEUM OF ART
HOLSTEBRO

In the twentieth century European artists rebelled against established traditions more violently and more widely than in any other comparable period of history. The expressions of revolt had a rich variety of names. Fauvism, cubism, futurism, orphism, expressionism, op art and pop art were only a few.

Some of the early revolt was directed against society as a whole rather than against artistic conventions. Dadaism, provoked by the appalling slaughter of World War I, was an expression of this.

The proper treatment of accepted standards, its adherents believed, was grotesque parody, even if it meant actions more readily associated with errant schoolchildren, such as painting a moustache on to a copy of the Mona Lisa.

Denmark was spared direct involvement in World War I, but steadily rather than violently, new artistic styles gained acceptance there. Most artistic fashions in the twentieth century tended indeed to be multinational, not least because of a revulsion against the excesses which nationalism had helped to bring about.

ASGER JORN

THE MOON DOG

CERAMIC

MUSEUM OF FINE ART

SILKEBORG

To gain an immediate impression of the strength and depth of the changes in Danish art styles it is necessary only to look at a Golden Age painting from the mid-nineteenth century and, a moment later, at one by a member of the Cobra group from the mid-twentieth. The contrast is richly revealing, though comparable transformations did of course take place in other European countries.

The revolution which French impressionism, followed by post-impressionism, had caused in European painting continued to be felt in Denmark in the early twentieth century. Not a few Danish painters were strongly influenced by Gauguin, even though Gauguin, who had a Danish wife, did not himself feel at ease in Denmark, finding its climate less congenial than that of the Pacific.

One who came temporarily under Gauguin's spell was J. F. Willumsen, an artist who attained such eminence in his lifetime that he was able to follow Thorvaldsen's example and make a public gift of his works on condition that a museum was built to house them. This came into being in Frederikssund on the Roskilde fjord, where his paintings, sculptures and work in other art forms can be seen as well as his fairly extensive collection of old masters.

Willumsen was a versatile and virile artist, an impressionist, a symbolist, a portrait-painter. Unlike many Danish painters he was drawn to mountains and, most strikingly in a work entitled "Nature Fear. After the Storm," could attribute a somewhat un-Danish savagery to natural forces. Largely because he spent much of his life abroad, with a preference for the south of France, he did not receive many commissions for portraits from Danish patrons. This is regrettable. In 1919 he was invited by the Museum of National History in Frederiksborg Castle to paint a portrait of Gustav Philipsen, a publisher and Copenhagen Councillor. The hope was expressed that the portrait would differ from those of other civic dignitaries, who wore black coats and "could just as well be undertakers."

The hope was fulfilled. Philipsen, placed against a yellow background, is wearing a mauve jacket. Reclining at obvious ease, with a short white beard, he gives the impression of being perceptive, humorous and understanding. No less impressive in a very different way is a portrait

painted by Willumsen fourteen years
later, and also in Frederiksborg. This is of
the actor Johannes Poulsen in the role of
Henry VIII of England in a play by Kaj
Munk. The portrait is, in a sense, a double
one, Poulsen appearing both as a rather
coarse-featured, powerful king and as the
producer who directs him in that role.

In the 1920s a small group of Danish
painters was established at Cagnes-sur-
Mer in southern France. Outstanding

J.F. Willumsen
Portrait of Gustav
Philipsen, publisher and
city councillor, "not an
undertaker"
Museum of National
History
Frederiksborg

among them was Vilhelm Lundstrøm, who experimented excitingly with abstract paintings, sculptures and collages in a manner which caused a group of physicians to declare him and some of his fellow-artists to be mentally ill.

The significance of an event which took place in 1933 was recognised only by a perceptive few. This was the coming together of a fairly homogeneous group of young artists determined to develop emerging styles in new and startling ways with all the excitement, rebellion and creativity which this involved. In these respects the event resembled, what had happened when Eckersberg had gathered his young followers round him.

The group was known as Linien or, in English, as The Line. Its first exhibition was held in Copenhagen in 1934, and twelve numbers of a publication of the same name appeared. The leader of the group and first editor of the magazine, Vilhelm Bjerke-Petersen, was only twenty-two, but he had already studied under Kandinsky and Klee and published a book entitled "Symbols in Abstract Art." At the age of nineteen he created a picture to be seen today in the Aarhus Art Museum entitled "Free Forms," which is a delightfully invigorating assembly of circular and semi-circular shapes.

Bjerke-Pedersen remained a dominant figure in various art movements,

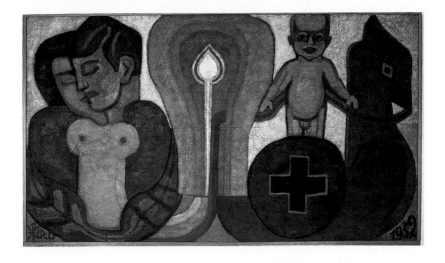

experimenting with symbolism,
surrealism and abstract expressionism, as
well as shadow-painting under the
influence of Magritte. The first number
of the magazine he edited contained an
article entitled "Symbol Language in Jazz
Cartoons" as well as some fairly
trenchant comments on contemporary
critics and on the Danish Royal Academy
of Fine Arts.

One of the most versatile members of
the group was Henry Heerup, who
enlivened the proceedings at the group's
first exhibition by riding round the
premises on a bicycle. Highly original
and difficult to classify, he made repeated
use of familiar objects, a heart, a cross or
a wheel, as symbols. His Madonnas are
highly original, and there is nothing
sacrilegious – there is indeed
considerable charm – in his Madonna on
an ironing-board. Whether making pen-
and-ink drawings, painting "scream

HENRY HEERUP

LIFECYCLE

MUSEUM OF ART

HOLSTEBRO

balloons" or carving an animal mother in granite, he conveyed an exhilarating zest for living.

Others of the group who were to rise to eminence included Ejler Bille and Richard Mortensen. Bille achieved distinction in more than one art form. One of his more haunting oil paintings has the revealing title "Symbols in Mobile Architecture." Much of his early work consisted of plastic sculptures. He had a nice wit and, incensed by the patronising comments of the daily press on Linien art, wrote a parody of them to describe the works of Rembrandt. His later paintings tend to convey a sense of quietness and depth, with dark colours, browns in particular, predominating. Mortensen, whose best work may be thought to belong to the second half of the century, enlivened the pages of the magazine with his pen-and-ink drawings.

International though the new styles predominantly were, a number of their practitioners retained a strong sense of national continuity. Mortensen, for instance, was a deep admirer of Abildgaard and wrote in Linien: "Danish painting is, first and foremost, objective: in fact, to borrow a modern term, functionalistic." A number of Linien artists made a combined study of frescoes in Danish medieval churches. Heerup looked for inspiration to Viking carvings in Jelling.

After Linien was closed down a comparable publication was launched with the title Helhesten. Literally this means "hell-horse," a three-footed creature of Scandinavian myth, which was associated with death.

The hell-horse was chosen because of contemporary events in other parts of Europe. The explosion of new art in Denmark coincided with the rise of Hitler to power in Germany, and in the years that followed there were strong political undertones in much of the work produced. "Art", Dr Goebbels declared in 1936, "would suffer no loss by the disappearance of the critic", and he thereupon issued instructions forbidding criticism of pictorial art, literature, music and drama. Danish artists understandably noted what was happening.

The German occupation of Denmark in the early 1940s gave rise to a number of paintings of undisguised protest. Among them were Hans

Scherfig's depiction of a prison cell in
Copenhagen and his Pied Piper of
Hamelin, in which a sinister piper leads
a group of would-be rebellious children
past a gibbet, from which two figures
are hanging.

VILHELM LUNDSTRØM
PACKING BOX PICTURE
LOUISIANA MUSEUM OF
MODERN ART

HENRY HEERUP
NAT OG DAG
MUSEUM OF ART
HOLSTEBRO

The outstanding Danish artists of the
wartime years were, for the most part,
those who had made their early impact
in the Linien and Helhesten movements.
One of them, steadily growing in stature,
was Asger Jorn, whose paintings were to
be among the great Danish creations in
the second half of the twentieth century.

Unifying forces among these artists were
advanced left-wing political views, a
belief in the need for spontaneity in
artistic creation, and a fascination with
masks of a kind which Picasso had also
felt. To some painters the masks seemed
to be a link with the arts of what were
considered "primitive" peoples. To others
they served as a means of conveying

more than one meaning. Asger Jorn's masks seemed to acquire a powerful identity of their own.

The collective name by which these painters are still known is Cobra, although, in fact, the name was applied to the group shortly before it lost its cohesion. By the end of World War II the more thoughtful Danish artists felt increasingly isolated, indeed peripheral, and contact was sought with artists of countries which had had similar experiences of occupation. The word "Cobra" was formed from the first letters of the names Copenhagen, Brussels and Amsterdam. In contrast with what had happened in earlier centuries Denmark was offering a lead to the Low Countries.

That the Cobra movement soon disintegrated was in part due to the naivete of the political beliefs of many of its adherents. These were set out in a manifesto which contained such statements as: "The culture of the individual, together with that of the class society from which it stems, is approaching its destruction." Cobra artists seem genuinely to have believed, at least for a time, that paint applied spontaneously would somehow bring them into direct contact with the masses. In fact they were themselves highly sophisticated artists who were – and perhaps still are – appreciated only by the discerning.

DETAIL

Fortunately their work is to be seen in Denmark today in a variety of museums. Among these is Louisiana in Humlebæk, where along a lengthy passage on the ground floor a number of works by Picasso and Giacometti are to be seen. Among them are paintings by Asger Jorn and Bille, Lundstrøm, Heerup and others of their contemporaries. The impartial observer may well feel that the blend is a happy and, in no ways, an incongruous one.

Two qualities are evident in much of the work of the best Danish painters before, during and immediately after World War II. One is energy, the other versatility. In not a few of their creations an explosion of paint on canvas seems to have taken place. The versatility is in part an expression of energy seeking outlets in a variety of art forms.

Heerup and Bille, though they saw themselves primarily as painters, were both sculptors of distinction. As such they were leaders of a revolt against the legacy of Thorvaldsen, which in the first half of the twentieth century may be thought to have persisted in Denmark for too long. French influence, particularly that of Rodin, is evident in the work of a number of Danish artists of the period who were primarily sculptors. One was Kaj Nielsen, another Gerhard Henning. In the carvings of both much of the appeal is in the gently erotic. Nielsen's Leda and the Swan, to be seen in the National Museum of Fine Arts in Copenhagen, is, in its smoothly curving lines, strongly reminiscent of some of the best known of Rodin's works.

A number of sculptors achieved success in the portrayal of beings chosen because they were unheroic figures. There was something of a revival of the classical tradition in the inter-war years, to which Einar Utzon-Frank, who long held the chair of sculpture at the Royal Fine Arts Academy, contributed powerfully. But the abstract and the surrealist tended to be most readily conceived and conveyed by artists practising in more than one discipline.

The versatility of certain creative artists in the twentieth century and their readiness to work in unfamiliar media were in time to have a widespread effect on the townscape of Denmark, on its museums and, most evidently, on objects in everyday use. This soon became apparent in

the production of glass. Denmark has no
long tradition of glass-making, among
the reasons for this being the lack of coal
for creating the necessary heat. For
decorative glass the rich had for centuries
turned to German and Czech craftsmen.
The first Danish glass-making factory
was established by the Countess
Henriette Danneskiold-Samsøe near the
Holmegaard peat-moor in Zealand as late
as 1825. Production for a long time was
largely of bottles and somewhat crude
phials, wine-glasses and other tableware.

HENRY HEERUP

DEATH REAPING

LOUISIANA MUSEUM OF

MODERN ART

A factory on the island of Fyn known as Fyns Glasværker produced some glass vases, lamps and containers in art nouveau style in the early years of the twentieth century. But glass production of distinction was to be seen mainly in the creations of the original factory established at Holmegaard. The factory today has a museum, whose exhibits are historically revealing. The early nineteenth century is represented by crude brown bottles, the first decorated glass dating from the 1920s. The production of such glass was a result of collaboration between the Holmegaard factory and Royal Copenhagen Porcelain.

The managing director of Royal Copenhagen had suggested that glass should be made in styles similar to those of the porcelain factory and that products of the two concerns should complement each other. A contract to this effect was signed in 1923, and the painter Oluf Jensen was commissioned to start work. His first glass had an engraved pattern similar to that of blue-fluted Copenhagen porcelain.

In 1929 an architect was appointed artistic director of the Holmegaard factory. He was Jacob Bang, who before long was creating sets of glasses numbering about a hundred pieces with names such as Violet and Primula. He made extensive use of smoky topaz glass, and before long Danish glass had begun to enjoy an international reputation. This reputation was to be hugely increased in the second half of the century. Bang aimed high, yet sought to make his glassware available to a wide public, advocating what he called "that honest frugality which should be the hall-mark of Danish products."

One of the most important appointments of an artist of distinction was made by the porcelain factory, Bing and Grøndahl, a powerful rival of Royal Copenhagen. This was its choice of J.F. Willumsen as its artistic director in 1897. Willumsen brought not only his skill as a sculptor to the creation of ceramic designs, but was enterprising enough to introduce new glazings and to revive the production of stoneware as an art form.

Bing and Grøndahl was later to be amalgamated with Royal Copenhagen, but it was during their period of rivalry that Danish ceramic styles attained new international distinction. This was shown by the award of the grand prix at the World Exhibition in Paris in 1900 for what was described as "the exhibition's most beautiful service," a product of Royal Copenhagen. For this blue had been sprayed in thin layers. Flowers were just visible on the edges of rims shaped like mussels. The design of the rims was said to be based on bumble-bees, dragon-flies and grasshoppers.

BLUE PHEASANT, FAIENCE
ROYAL COPENHAGEN

Another expression of international esteem was to be found in the 1911 edition of the Encyclopaedia Britannica, which stated of the products of Royal Copenhagen that they "are not only famous all over the world, but have set a new style in porcelain decoration which is being followed at most of the Continental factories." The writer added: "The Royal Copenhagen works have also produced a profusion of skilfully modelled animals, birds and fishes, either in pure white or tinted after nature, with the same underglaze colours. Other European factories have adopted the modern Copenhagen style of decoration."

POLAR BEAR
ROYAL COPENHAGEN

The influence of Arnold Krog, ardent admirer of Japanese designs, continued to be felt within Royal Copenhagen in the early years of the twentieth century, but there was a growing tendency, as the Encyclopaedia Britannica made clear, to look for inspiration to the animal and peasant life of Denmark. Gulls and swans, mallards and owls were among subjects treated. The proximity of the Copenhagen zoo was thought to have

given rise to the abundance of polar
bears in Danish porcelain. One
perceptive critic even asked whether
there was any other factory in the world
which could produce a porcelain turkey
being directed, together with her brood,
from a garden up a staircase.

A kingfisher, his beak pointing towards
the sky, by Peter Herold, a puzzled
Siamese cat by Theodor Madsen and a
contented cocker spaniel by Svend
Jespersen were among the creations of
the inter-war years.

Hans Christian Andersen characters from
such stories as The Soldier and the
Witch and The Tinder Box provided
ready inspiration, as did children and

VASE DESIGNED BY EFFIE
HEGERMANN-LINDENCRONE
FOR BING AND GRØNDAHL

peasant women chosen from real life. A disciplined respect for line, in preference, if necessary, to colour, remained evident, yet it is difficult to escape the conclusion that in Danish porcelain of the period birds and bears, and indeed the familiar Flora Danica, received more skilful treatment than did the human race.

In the first half of the century too, following the amalgamation of Royal Porcelain and the Aluminia factory, there was a resurgence of faience and earthenware production of some distinction. Harlequins, Columbines and characters from A Midsummer Night's Dream, ranging from Titania to Bottom, Oberon to Puck, were among the most sought-after products. Some of the best faience was the work of the painter Christian Joachim, who created the service known as Blue Pheasant and who, in much of his work, used a tulip motif.

The revival of stoneware attracted a number of distinguished artists, among them Paul Gauguin's son, Jean. A wide range of materials, including copper and iron, basalt and uranium, were used to provide rich colours, such as plum and violet, and variegated shapes.

Of all the forms of industrial production which create objects of beauty the one in which Denmark made the most startling advances in the early years of the twentieth century was silverware.

HANS CHRISTIAN ANDERSEN

In this one man played a leading role. He was Georg Jensen, who has been described as "the greatest silversmith of our century." Indeed in its obituary notice the New York Herald Tribune described him as "the greatest craftsman in silver for the last three hundred years."

Jensen was the son of a grinder employed in a knife factory. He was apprenticed to a jeweller, then studied sculpture at the Royal Academy of Fine Art. In his early thirties he decided that his future was to be as a silversmith, and in 1904 he opened his own workshop. "Silver," he was later to declare, "is the best material we have. It has this exquisite moonlight shimmer, the glimmer of Danish summer evenings." His early work was influenced by art nouveau designs, but before long he developed his own individual style,

SILVER JUG

which was, throughout his career, based
on his respect for silver. Large plain
surfaces served to reveal the beauty of
the material, and contrast could be
provided by decorative details with fruit
or leaf motifs, perhaps a stylised flower or
a cluster of grapes.

He exploited too the softness of silver to
create swelling forms and to reflect light
from barely perceptible hammer-marks.
Through oxidisation a deep, soft whitish-
grey shade was achieved with a matt
finish. His range was extensive, and some
of his cutlery services had more than two
hundred pieces.

Soon after he opened his workshop
Jensen engaged the services of Johan
Rohde, a painter, who was also a
furniture designer of some distinction.

SILVER JUG

Rohde created for Jensen a variety of bowls and other tableware of a greater simplicity than Jensen himself favoured. Simplicity was to be taken further in the work of Kay Bojesen, who served his apprenticeship.

By the 1930s Bojesen had effectively rebelled against Jensen's style and tradition. He abandoned Jensen's hammering technique and sought gentleness of line rather than decoration. "Lines," he declared, "should be friendly. The things we make should have life and heart in them and be a joy to hold." In preference to the surfaces which Jensen created he delighted in the lustre and reflection of burnished silver. The pleasure derived from silver objects in everyday use, he believed, was enhanced by the marks created by wear and tear, and it was by regular polishing that the surfaces admired in old silver were obtained.

Jensen was the great pioneer who revived the craft of the silversmith in Denmark. The name "Jensen" has become almost synonymous with Danish silver, and in shops bearing that name an abundance of fine work can be seen today. But it was Bojesen and his immediate followers, such as Magnus Stephensen, who established the styles of the mid-twentieth century, from which new and exciting departures were to be made.

Examples of Bojesen's own work which attracted international attention included two silver bowls exhibited in the United States in 1953. They were of total simplicity and placed on rosewood platters, reflecting light and shade in a manner which viewers found compulsive.

In architecture Denmark was comparatively slow to adopt the functionalism which was indulged in with such enthusiasm by the avant-garde in some other European countries. Indeed even after acceptance there was a tendency to retain such traditional features as tiled roofs and red bricks.

Recognition of the merits of new styles coincided, to some extent, with the rise to prominence of Arne Jacobsen, who was born in 1902. In 1929 he produced, in collaboration with a young friend, Flemming Lassen, the winning design in a competition entitled "The House of the Future." Their design was not only of the building itself, but of its interior decoration, its furniture and its textiles. This was a foretaste of the

versatility Jacobsen was to show in his
long career. The house was round in
shape, with suggestions of spiralling.
Tubular steel and glass were used in the
furnishings, and there was even a
landing-pad on the roof for an auto-giro.

Jacobsen's early understanding of how
architecture could be adapted to meet
changes in social habits can be clearly
seen in the Bellavista housing scheme
and the nearby Bellevue theatre complex
in Copenhagen, which were completed
between the years 1932 and 1935. The
housing structure, although having the
appearance of concrete, is in fact of
stuccoed brick. The balconies, looking
out over the sea, appear, not as additions,
but as integral parts of the whole. The
buildings designed include beach-huts
and lifeguard towers. The theatre was
planned primarily as a setting for
summer revues.

Other creations of Jacobsen before and in
the early years of World War II included
Aarhus town hall, which he designed in
collaboration with Erik Møller. Its
horizontal and vertical slabs of reinforced
concrete and unconventional tower,
happily accepted today, were highly
controversial when first revealed to a
startled public.

Another town hall of the same period,
that at Lyngby, was also too exciting not
to be controversial. Designed by Martin
Jensen and Hans Langkilde, it was built

WALL PAINTING DETAILS
AARHUS TOWN HALL

of reinforced concrete, with facades in Greenland marble and a copper-covered penthouse. Concave in shape and with five floors, it has lines of no little beauty.

Controversial when it was completed, controversial today and unquestionably impressive is a Copenhagen church, which was constructed over a period covering nearly all the inter-war years. It was built as a memorial to the distinguished priest and poet, N. F. S. Grundtvig, and was perhaps most aptly described by its architect, Peder Jensen-Klint, as an oversized village church. Gothic elements are evident in the facade, with new forms of stepping-stones pointing towards a familiar Heaven. There are three aisles, and the building material is all yellow brick. Not the least of the church's attractions are the light effects in the interior, which are strangely ethereal.

Jacobsen's international fame came in the post-war years, not least through buildings which he created overseas, such as the Danish Embassy in London. In those same years Danish architects were to achieve world-wide recognition of a kind which the nation had not known before. They did so through partnership with industry in the building of airports and factories, hotels and bridges. They did so too, in accordance with an older Danish tradition, by the creation of a wealth of village churches.

ARCHITECT

PEDER JENSEN KLINT

CHURCH DEDICATED TO

N. F. S. GRUNDTVIG,

DISTINGUISHED POET

AND PRIEST

COPENHAGEN

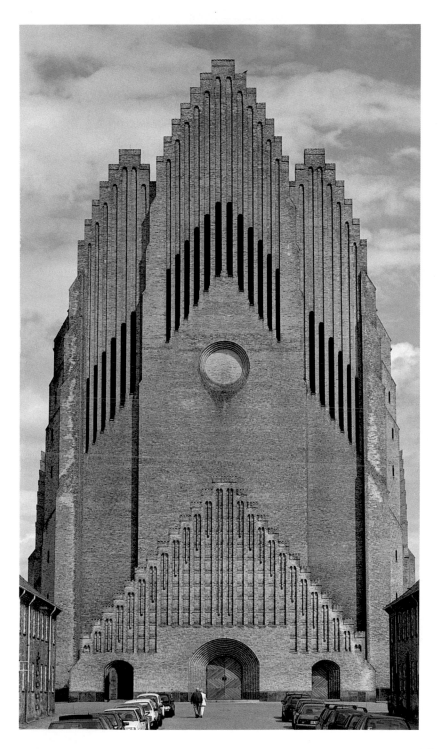

VIII.

TRIUMPH OF DESIGN

TWO WOMEN LOOKING OVER
BALUSTRADE. BRONZE
COPENHAGEN AIRPORT

"Could beauty, my lord, have better company than with honesty?" – Ophelia, Hamlet

The visitor's introduction to the visual arts of Denmark is likely to begin at Copenhagen airport. The first buildings were constructed in the 1920s. In the 1990s major changes were made, based on the designs of the architectural firm Holm and Grut.

Curved shapes evoke the wings of aircraft. Roofs are supported by columns which spread like branches of trees and disappear into ceilings. There is a floor mosaic of black granite and white marble. Arched ceilings reflect surfaces intended to suggest Nordic light. Visual contact with the aircraft outside is maintained.

Perhaps the most exciting part of the whole design is the multi-coloured glasswork created by Per Steen Habsgaard in collaboration with the Norwegian

painter Frans Widerberg. Their horse and horseman, constructed of eighteen elements, occupy a commanding position, where two piers join.

Initiation into the visual arts continues through street and shop, office and hotel. Gradually the eye becomes aware of the pleasure to be derived from the shape, or perhaps lustre, of balconies and beer-glasses, lettering and lampshades, vending machines, chair legs and reception desks.

PER STEEN HABSGAARD AND
FRANS WIDERBERG
GLASS FIGURE OF HORSE AND
RIDER
COPENHAGEN AIRPORT

Denmark in the late twentieth century has become a country in which
supply and demand of good design seem to complement each other.
Standards set by industry and commerce are high, and there is an evident
wealth of good designers to meet these demands in a wide and increasing
range of materials.

Among those whose designs may most immediately impress visitors are
the creators of museums, in which many of the treasures of Denmark are
now displayed. Denmark has a museum tradition of some distinction. The
Rosenborg and Thorvaldsen displays were revolutionary in their times.
One of the world's leading authorities on preservation within museums
was a Dane, Gustav Rosenberg. In the second half of the twentieth
century new levels of excellence were attained, Louisiana, which lies a
little north of Copenhagen, pointing in directions where others would
follow.

The creators of Louisiana, mainly the architects Bo and Wohlert, clearly
intended it to be a place which it would be a delight to visit, irrespective
of any pleasure derived from looking at paintings. The main buildings are
set in a garden, with distinguished statuary scattered around, seemingly
casually. The passage with the Picassos and the Cobra paintings leads
directly into a large, bright cafe, from which the outlook is on to grass
leading down to the sea. The roof suggests a ship under full sail, and
across the water lies Sweden.

To countless visitors, used to climbing steep, wide stairs in uninviting
light to see the world's masterpieces placed against drab-coloured walls,
with uniformed attendants hovering menacingly, Louisiana has been a
revelation.

Novelty of concept has too resulted in excellence of design in the
Trapholt Museum, near Kolding, which was opened in 1988. This too has
a rural setting, with a garden on one side and half-timbered houses on
the other. While walking through the galleries viewers are momentarily
diverted by a vista of a fjord.

A startling impact is made at the entrance to the museum by the
harlequinade of colours in the statuary of Egon Fischer. Some corridors

are curved and lined with ceramics on
window-sills. Elsewhere movement is up
and down steps in a series of surprises.
A large central feature is a gallery, two
storeys high, devoted to the abstract
paintings of Richard Mortensesn, who
collaborated closely with the architect,
Boje Lundgaard, in its design.

Modern museums of outstanding quality
are to be found in various parts of
Denmark. One such is the Museum of
Art in Aarhus, which has a rich
collection of Danish paintings and
sculpture, and where novel techniques
have been used to minimise the
differences between artificial and
natural light.

LOUISIANA INTERIOR
GALLERY WITH WORKS BY
COBRA ARTISTS
LOUISIANA MUSEUM OF
MODERN ART

MACAW BOWL ON BEACH
BORNHOLM

GLASS BOWL AMONG FOLIAGE
BORNHOLM

TWO EXAMPLES OF BALTIC
SEA GLASS BY
MAI BRITT JÖNSSON AND
PETE HUNNER

As in Louisiana, an art gallery was constructed in the likeness of an ocean-going vessel in Køge bay, to the south of Copenhagen. Its name, Arken, means "The Ark", and its main axes form parallels to the sea and the harbour. A large central space, 150 metres long, with light grey walls, is intended to induce peace and reflection in contrast with the bright white of the adjoining galleries.

The practice of devoting a museum largely to the art of a single Danish artist, begun by Thorvaldsen, has continued, one outstanding example being at Silkeborg, where it is possible to enjoy rich helpings of the works of Asger Jorn.

The new museums show for the most part contemporary or near-contemporary work, but in the late 1990s an ambitious plan was put into effect for the transformation of the building housing the great collection of national and international art through the ages, the National Museum of Fine Arts (Statens Museum for Kunst) in Copenhagen.

The original building, dating from 1895, is set in a park, and one of the terms of the competition for a design of an additional structure was that the main building's situation and symmetry must both be respected.

The structure which emerged, slim, detached from the main building and set on pillars, gives the impression of floating

on trees in the background. The
architects, C.F. Møller and Partners,
advocates of simplicity in design and the
use of local materials, already had to their
credit art museums in Aarhus and
Herning. Transformation of the interior
was on a comparable scale, one outcome
of the rebuilding being that not a single
work was placed where it had been
before reconstruction began.

Concurrently with the widespread
creation of new buildings to house works
of art has come a surge of creative activity
in diversified forms. Indeed some
communities in Denmark seem today to
revolve largely around such activity. One
is to be found on the island of Bornholm.

ELSE LETH-NISSEN
GLASS BOWL
BORNHOLM

Bornholm has developed, to some
extent, in isolation from the rest of
Denmark. Its medieval round churches
had unique qualities, and a tradition was
established of self-help as a community.
In the second half of the twentieth
century extensive rebuilding was
needed, following Soviet bombing of
the island when it had been under
German occupation.

Among the striking new buildings
were a number of wooden houses of
varied colour patterns, which were a
gift from Sweden, and an art museum.
The museum has an impressive range
of works produced within a
community which numbers only some
45,000 people.

ELSE LETH-NISSEN
BLUE GLASS BOWL
BORNHOLM

Some of the most exciting work has been done in glass. In the late 1970s the conductor of the Malmö orchestra, Mogens Dam, suggested that a number of herring smokehouses, which had fallen into disuse. might be converted into glass factories. This was done, and within about a decade four new glass and ceramics works were in operation. Upwards of a hundred creative artists, a number of them from overseas, were at work. In the northern part of Bornholm there are now more art galleries than there are bakeries.

Among the more memorable works in glass are those of Pernille Bulow, who has achieved some extraordinary contrasts in glass: yellow on blue, blue on yellow, gold on ultramarine.

The techniques adopted by Else Leth-Nissen in etching and sand-blasting have resulted in rhythmic, dancing patterns involving birds and foliage.

Sculptors and silversmiths, weavers and leather-workers are all to be found engaged in creative work on this island of 45,000 people. There are, too, inventive and original artists giving new distinction to Danish ceramics, but it is glass that has brought Bornholm its international distinction. The claim has even been made that it is now more than merely a contender with Murano, the Adriatic island which has for long been the home of Venetian glass.

ANJA KJÆR
HARLEQUIN
ROYAL COPENHAGEN CRYSTAL

MICHAEL BANG
GLASS BOWLS
HOLMEGAARD GLASS

In the 1960s, following a merger with
its main rivals, Fyn and Kastrup, the
Holmegaard works became even more
important as a centre of large-scale
manufacture of glass for domestic use.
Its principal designer for more than fifty
years after his appointment in 1942 was
Per Lütken.

Lütken's natural inclinations were
somewhat conservative. He had a deep
love for thick, soft, colourless glass
which could be moulded into rounded
forms. One of his creations in the 1960s
was the Pearl set, in which the glass was
trimmed without being cut and in
which no two pieces were identical.
Later he indulged more in colour, his
shapes became more adventurous, and
he developed new production methods.
One of these involved the turning of a
lump of hot glass in an iron, bowl-
shaped mould.

In 1992, fifty years after his appointment
as chief designer, Lütken created a bowl
of extraordinary delicacy, which
somehow seems to be in perpetual
motion. It was in this direction that his
natural successors tended to move. One
of them was Torben Jørgensen, who
stated: "Glass is a living material, which
likes to flow and set its own course."
Among the flowing objects he created
were tall, slender glasses, decanters with
blue tops, and paperweights, inside
which were small objects shaped like
golf-balls and painted blue and gold.

MICHAEL BANG

GLASS BOWL AND COVER

HOLMEGAARD GLASS

The succession was continued by Anja Kjær, creator of so-called harlequin shapes in turquoise and violet glass, and maker of glasses for the Queen of Denmark's silver wedding. These were exciting creations, with curves inside and a dotted pattern on the exterior.

Further amalgamations led to the union of Royal Copenhagen with manufacturers in other materials. One of these was the court jewellers, A. Michelsen, an early outcome being the creation of a range of jewels in which porcelain has been combined with precious metals. Another merger was with the famous Jensen firm of silversmiths. All these concerns, as well as Holmegaard glass, eventually came under the financial umbrella of Carlsberg in what has proved to be a successful, perhaps uniquely successful, union of art and commerce.

In the second half of the twentieth century Royal Copenhagen has retained its characteristic blend of conservatism and novelty. In its central factory girls can be seen today, with paint and pattern-book in front of them, creating for the well-to-do purchaser the same wealth of Scandinavian flora on porcelain which was once intended for the Empress Catherine of Russia. A thousand brush-strokes continue to fashion a blue-fluted plate. Animals in porcelain continue to emerge, with inquisitive pandas and predatory salmon-trout added to the range of species.

There are exciting novelties too. Among them are the vases with circular patterns of Henning Koppel, artist of distinction in glass and silver as well as ceramics; the porcelain tiles of Jørn Larsen; the vases suggestive of abstract sculptures of Bjørn Nørgaard.

The feeling that a talented and highly original sculptor has been at work may well come too from contemplation of the best new Jensen silverware: knives and teapots, brooches, bracelets and purely ornamental figures.

That modern Danish artists working with a variety of more or less plastic materials have created work of outstanding distinction can hardly be disputed. Whether this has or has not been matched, or surpassed, by those whom the world knows primarily as painters may be for posterity to decide.

In 1984 an exhibition of Nordic art was staged in New York. The three painters featured were Edvard Munch, Asger Jorn and the young Per Kirkeby. This was indicative of the judgment of the artistic world outside Scandinavia.

Those who have grown familiar with his work may well see Asger Jorn as something of a giant. As a young man shortly before the outbreak of World War II he had the good fortune to be a pupil of Fernand Léger. After his association with Cobra he returned to live for a time in France, his best work, it may well be thought, dating from that period. As an artist he was versatile and prolific, working with paint, stone, ceramics and tapestry. Attracted early in his life to surrealism and the abstract, he studied with care Danish and other Nordic Viking and medieval art. He had a wide interest in the work of his contemporaries. When he made a donation to the Silkeborg Museum of more than 5,000 works by himself and others some 150 artists were represented.

He was continually ready to experiment. A fellow artist, the photographer Poul Pedersen, on one occasion suggested that they should try making drawings with light in front of an open camera. Jorn used his light to fashion drawings of different thicknesses, with dots and gaps produced by switching the light off and on. The results served as the basis of a number of major paintings to be seen today in the Aarhus Museum of Art.

TORBEN JØRGENSEN
GLASS SCULPTURE
ROYAL COPENHAGEN

The immediate impressions which a painting by Jorn are likely to make on the viewer are of vigour, variety, spontaneity and, in a number of works, explosive force. Among his best known creations are a huge Stalingrad and a painting entitled Letter to My Son, in which, out of a lava-like flow of paint on canvas, a toy fire engine can be seen emerging.

A fellow-artist, Egill Jacobsen, once wrote of him: "If we want to understand Asger Jorn, we must go out into the vast, cosmic night, where small creatures, many small creatures, are fighting an incessant battle in order to become participants in the great drama which will always be inevitable for those who are seers. In his pictures he has been aggressive in his search for content in expression. That is why he touches new strings."

Jorn died in 1973. By then the political naivete which had characterised much of the Cobra movement had ceased to be in vogue, and rebellion and the search for something new in painting had taken other forms. Minimalist art, American pop art and early experiments in conceptual art all had their Danish adherents.

There were various painted protests against the power of technology in modern society. An exhibition called The Upside-Down Knife featured the work

ALBERT MERTZ

EXPLOSION

MUSEUM OF FINE ART

HOLSTEBRO

of a number of talented young artists, who covered walls and ceilings with paint to express what was called the post-modern condition. That they became publicly known as "the savages" did not deter them. So long as protest was in vogue it was not altogether surprising that Bjørn Nørgaard, a sculptor of no little distinction, accompanied by one artist dressed as a priestess carrying a black cross and another playing a violin, could publicly slaughter a horse in a field to call attention to what was happening in Vietnam.

Amid the froth, the ephemeral and the youthful idealism, which are all part of the excitement of novel movements in art, new treasures of Denmark may well be thought to have emerged, notably in the work of Per Kirkeby.

ASGER JORN
DEAD DRUNK DANES
LOUISIANA MUSEUM OF
MODERN ART

Kirkeby, who was born in 1938, was a student at the so-called
Experimental School of Art and was early attracted to minimalism. His
own experiments included collage and the use of hardboard instead of
canvas and synthetic lacquers instead of paint. He learnt much during
stays in Karlsruhe and Berlin, particularly from the discipline he imposed
on himself in making numerous drawings in order to achieve the clarity
he sought. His paintings of this period have been likened to landscape and
sky immediately following a violent thunderstorm.

He soon achieved international distinction when he was still in his
thirties, at the Venice Biennale, and later at a one-man show in Essen.
Recognition in Denmark came quite suddenly, and when it did he had
already established a distinctive style of his own.

Kirkeby is a serious geologist. He took part in an expedition to north
Greenland and later used the knowledge he had acquired to paint
landscapes with no horizons, but with rich colour and a variety of areas of
water, fungi, stones and trees. Of his landscapes he wrote that they are
"marked by a certain light that is Danish or Nordic."

He is also a film-maker and prolific writer in prose and poetry and, in the
visual arts, a bold experimenter. Gradually the figurative element tended
to disappear from his paintings, and he became more and more interested
in the creation of brick structures, which he described as "buildings with
no function". For a major exhibition of his work, which was staged at the
Tate Gallery in London in 1995, he created a large structure of this kind,
which divided a portion of the gallery and determined to a considerable
extent the ways in which the paintings could be viewed.

There is an abundance of modern Danish painting to be seen today, not
only in museums and art galleries, but also on the walls of buildings in
city streets and in the foyers of not a few hotels. Visitors can in
consequence roam widely in search of the treasures which may be found
among them.

Some will look, no doubt, to the colour combinations of Richard
Mortensen and the sense of movement they arouse. Others will be struck
by the vigour and versatility with which Wilhelm Freddie causes human

figures to be confronted by a variety of
objects and abstracts, a few mocking,
others menacing.

Some will be impressed by the vast
landscapes of Nina Sten-Knudsen with
wolves outlined by neon writing, others
by the manner in which Troels Wørsel has
translated into practice his theory that
painting is like making gravy. Gravy, he
pointed out, is something liquid, sieved
and transported to a saucepan, altering
form and undergoing other
transformations.

Some will admire the dots and dashes
and collage surrounding the human
figures of Erik Frandsen, others the
paintings fashioned by Peter Rønde with
silver paper and straw. Among the most
popular painted objects have been those

PER KIRKEBY
MUCH LATER
LOUISIANA MUSEUM OF
MODERN ART

PER KIRKEBY
APOCALYPSE
LOUISIANA MUSEUM OF
MODERN ART

of Jens Birkemos, creator, among much else, of fabulous beasts which were to decorate the shopping-bags of a highly successful supermarket.

Much of all this is the outcome of painstaking labour. In an age of widespread and ingenious experimentation examples can also be found of the kind of artefact which caused the Czech writer, Milan Kundera, to describe the appearance of New York as "beauty by mistake".

Kirkeby's amalgamation of painting and brick structure was indicative of trends in much Danish art in the second half of the twentieth century. With the use of new methods and new materials painting has veered towards the three-dimensional, sometimes reaching the point at which the artist becomes painter-sculptor. As sculptors became more ambitious some of their creations tended, like Kirkeby's brick walls, to be regarded as buildings. In turn architecture has blended with street furniture, not only in such traditional forms as the fountain, but in the development of the townscape as a whole,

A spectacular blending of painting and sculpture is to be seen, for example, in the work of Stig Brøgger, whose Upupa-Epos, embracing a variety of forms, was described as an allegorical tale in thirty-six pictures. In Double Sculpture he aimed at creating what he called a total environment to express much of the complexity of the world.

In 1974 Brøgger and two fellow-artists, Hem Heinsen and Mogens Møller, formed the so-called Institute for Scale Art in an attempt to bridge the gap between conventional art forms and other kinds of production. A few years later they collaborated in creating for Aalborg University a huge iron star, which emerges from a circular pile of stones, the whole project being conceived on what was described as "a landscape scale."

Among Heinsen's most striking works is his Standing Sculpture, in which three spirals, one based on the cylinder, one on the cube and one an amorphous mass, rise from the ground entangled one in another. In his sculpture entitled St Sebastian the figure of the saint is missing, but a large sheet of sand-blown glass, placed between plywood boards, is pierced by a profusion of arrows.

Møller, who felt that his break with minimalist art had had a liberating effect, carved a figure in somewhat classical style placed between an egg, symbolising the origin of life, and a coffin. His sculpture, Pioneer, was first executed in wood, the final version being in steel. The pioneer is an explorer only in the mind, as he is seated in a cramped position, possibly in front of a television screen. His body is deformed and his features indeterminate.

Among the more disturbing late twentieth century Danish sculptures are those of Michael Kvium, whose concern with death, deformities and natural catastrophes is manifest. In one work entitled Future Jam a variety of naked infants with large heads are interspersed with coils of rope. By contrast a near contemporary of Kvium's, Margrete Sørensen, who was born in 1949, conveys feelings of openness and hope. She makes repeated use of the spiral, and in one of her works a pyramid is adorned by a Jacob's ladder. She even uses semi-circular plates surrounded by red and suggestive of a human heart,

The sculptor whose work the uninstructed visitor may most readily assume to be a building rather than a carving is surely Bjørn Nørgaard, the man who slaughtered a horse in protest against the war in Vietnam. His best known work, The Human Wall, after being displayed in New York, Philadelphia and Los Angeles, was placed in 1984 in front of the National Museum of Fine Arts in Copenhagen.

The wall, constructed of concrete, wood, stoneware and bronze, seems to open like a fan. The human figures are alive, sensuous and seductive. The colours are exuberant, and there are contorted spirals at the extremes. Various myths are portrayed, and the central figure is a young Scandinavian girl voyaging through history and culture.

Nørgaard was a master in the use of contrasting materials. This is evident in his Cupola, fashioned from copper, iron, marble, glass and various kinds of glue. He could incorporate tradition and not simply rebel

against it, as perhaps too many of his contemporaries did. Indeed he even described his work, disparagingly, as "popular, recycled classicism." More aptly he stated on another occasion that the driving force in his work was "man's interest in man."

Just as the work of Asger Jorn extended over the years both before and after World

ASGER JORN
EUPHORISM
MUSEUM OF FINE ART
SILKEBORG

War II, so too did that of Arne Jacobsen.
Features of his domestic architecture in
the 1950s were yellow brick and sloping
roofs. After a time right angles, smooth
surfaces and the use of glass, became
increasingly evident. His interiors were
more spacious and the furniture he
designed had a sculptural quality.

Among his best known buildings in
Denmark is the Radisson SAS Royal
Hotel in Copenhagen, in which his
involvement was total. Not only did he

RADISSON SAS
SCANDINAVIA HOTEL,
AARHUS

design the building and its original furniture, but he concerned himself with small constructional details. He was influenced by the American skyscraper, but he was determined that the new building should not dominate the skyline. In this he was extraordinarily successful. Although the hotel has twenty storeys, the light colours and the reflection from glass seem to blend happily with the Danish light. Alterations have been made in the interior, but the sense of unity and space created in the lobby and adjoining restaurants and bars has been happily preserved.

Much modern hotel design in Denmark is of a high order. An exciting example is the Scandinavia in Aarhus, also one of the Radisson SAS group. Much of it, including the glass lifts with views and the glass bridges linking corridors, gives the impression of a modern Crystal Palace.

Adjoining the hotel is a concert hall built to the prize-winning design in a competition staged in 1977. Unlike the kind of concert hall which is open to the public only when performances are taking place, the new building was designed to attract visitors at all times of the day and the year. One wall in the foyer is largely covered with a painting by Richard Mortensen, and there is a permanent collection of modern Danish art as well a 1500 square metre space for temporary exhibitions.

DETAIL OF RADISSON SAS
SCANDINAVIA HOTEL,
AARHUS

SVEND HANSEN
MAN MEETS THE SEA
ESBJERG

A condition of the 1977 competition was that the building should form an integrated whole with the park surrounding Aarhus City Hall. Palm trees and olive trees in the foyer, maintained by skilful temperature control, and a shallow pool outside serve to achieve this effect.

The concept of a public building which serves almost as an impromptu art gallery may perhaps be considered characteristic of modern architecture in Aarhus. The architect of the new University building, C. F. Møller, was a strong advocate of giving prominence to sculpture and painting. The University has expanded hugely since Møller began work, but the principle of incorporating other art forms has been happily maintained.

Jacobsen's last major work in Denmark
was his design of the National Bank in
Copenhagen, which replaced a
Florentine-style palace. The detailed plan
of the new building is said to be kept
secret for security reasons. What can be
seen includes an enormously high ceiling,
a delicate-looking glass and steel stairway,
a floor fashioned from white marble
gravel, several courtyards and roof gardens.

A feature of Danish towns, small and
large, which must surely impress the
visitor, is the wealth of modern open-air
sculpture, a wealth which even extends
here and there to the countryside.

Some of it is on a massive scale. In
Esbjerg, for instance, a town whose
drama and music centre centre was
designed by Utzon, four human figures,
some nine metres high, dominate the
coastline to the north of the harbour.
The sculptor, Svend Hansen, gave it the
title Man Meets the Sea.

On the narrow island of Langeland,
which lies between Fyn and Zealand, an
enterprise known as TICKON was
established, largely through the initiative
of Alfio Bonanno, a Sicilian, who settled
on the island in 1970. TICKON is an
abbreviation for a Danish title meaning
International Centre for Art and Nature.
Under the Centre's guidance numerous ·
sculptures in stone, wood and bone have
been placed among trees and marshes
and lakes.

DETAIL, MAN MEETS THE SEA

Sculpture parks with a startling variety of work are to be found in a number of Danish towns. The park in Aalborg contains Nørgaard's Dream Palace. The park in Herning has six granite sculptures by Heerup as well as Robert Jacobsen's Robin Hood and structures in materials ranging from bronze to glass-fibre.

Elsewhere walks among sculptures created wholly, or predominantly, in the second half of the twentieth century can be enjoyed virtually without interruption. In Sæby a tuba-player, a stone age man and a family group carved in black Swedish granite are among the subjects treated. In Nykøbing they include a crow's head and a stairway to Heaven.

In Holstebro the placing of a Giacometti figure in front of the entrance to the town's leading hotel was followed by a variety of outdoor sculptures. An impressive new town hall, divided from an equally impressive public library has a courtyard dominated by sculpture, followed. With a wealth of paintings, a ballet and a theatre, Holstebro, a town of some 40,000 inhabitants, invites the question: where else can a town of this size be found in which modern art plays such a predominant part?

A walk through Odense will bring the visitor face to face with a striking statue of Icarus and, perhaps more

Astrid Noack, Bronze
Kneeling Boy
Holstebro

significantly, with a variety of characters created by Hans Christian Andersen. This surely is a unique compliment paid by a city to its most famous son. The visitor who goes shopping in Stratford-on-Avon or St Petersburg or Florence will not be confronted by Romeo and Juliet or Anna Karenina or characters from the Divina Commedia. Andersen once said: "I covet honour in the same way as the miser covets gold." In the streets of Odense he has it in perpetuity.

Denmark differs from many countries in that tax laws have enabled commercial enterprises to engage in the kind of large housing schemes which are normally the preserve of a municipal authority. One such scheme, brought into being in the early 1990s, is the Dalgas Have project in Copenhagen. The principal architect was Henning Larsen, a man who has fashioned beauty in a variety of architectural forms in Denmark. White, symmetrical, somewhat formal, indeed classical, the complex has sixteen tower-blocks, yet remains restful, rather than intrusive, on the eye.

Other housing schemes in the Copenhagen area include Hyldespjældet, where the differing heights and colouring of the facades create an almost Mediterranean effect, and the waterside Paustians Hus in Østerbro, which is characterised by columns, not only of varying heights, but of varying spaces in between. The creator of the Paustians

PAUL CEDERDORFF
RECLINING WOMAN
HOLSTEBRO

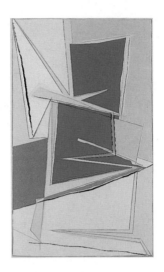

RICHARD MORTENSEN
EVISA
LOUISIANA MUSEUM OF
MODERN ART

Hus, Jørn Utzon, who was born in 1918, may well be considered the greatest Danish architect of his time.

A number of Danish architects in the twentieth century have enjoyed international reputations. What is little known outside Denmark is that some of their best work has been the design of new churches. Utzon is one of whom this is true, Henning Larsen another. That the churches were built was largely due to legislation permitting public funds to be used for new church construction.

Utzon is known to the outside world as the creator of the Sydney Opera House and, to a lesser extent, as the architect of the new parliament building in Kuwait. In Denmark his greatest masterpiece may well be considered Bagsværd church. The essence of Utzon's triumph in Bagsværd is the use or, as it seems, the creation of light. The main structure is of light-coloured concrete, and glazed tiles on the facade match the concrete's covering. The roof above the arch of the church has an aluminium covering. The altar is also of concrete, with screens of white-painted brick behind it. The woodwork is of pine.

His preliminary sketches indicate the effects which Utzon sought to achieve and did achieve. They show a congregation beneath clouds, through which a heavenly light is breaking. The cloud effect is created largely through the undulating concrete ceiling.

Some of the finest modern Danish churches are to be found in small towns and villages. In Strandby, near Frederikshavn, a community of some 3,000 people largely dependent on fishing, two sisters who lived on a farm left all their money for the building of a new church. Public funds were added, and Jakob Blagvard was appointed architect. The church is whitewashed, with curves suggestive of fishing-boats.

BJØRN NØRGAARD
THE SPIRAL
LOUISIANA MUSEUM
OF MODERN ART

HENNING LARSEN
INTERIOR
ENGHØJ CHURCH

In the north windows, where Old Testament scenes are depicted, the dominant colours are green and blue. In the south windows, devoted to the New Testament, they are mainly red and yellow.

Henning Larsen, who was at one time a pupil of Jacobsen's and who first achieved international renown by winning a competition for the design of the new university in Trondheim in Norway, enriched the small community of Enghøj in Jutland with a church of compelling beauty.

The entrance is past earthworks, which create the impression of burial mounds, then through a plain black door. The first object which strikes the eye appears to be the wooden keel of a ship, giving the visitor a momentary sensation of being under water. Light streams in from behind the altar, and the eye is irresistibly drawn to the small, plain, black crucifix which stands on it. There it may well rest in wonder, to be readily followed by prayer.

These pages have told of some of the treasures of Denmark. Why the treasures are so little known in other countries is an intriguing mystery. Perhaps there is a need for some new Vikings of the spirit to convey treasures across the waves, not the waves the old Vikings conquered, but the new waves so abundant today.

HENNING LARSEN
ENGHØJ CHURCH

INDEX

Pictures are indicated by italicised page numbers.

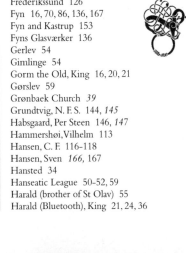

PICTURE CREDITS